CLINT EASTWOOD

by the same author

Belmondo (in collaboration with Stéphane Lévy-Klein), Editions PAC, 1975.
Paul Newman, Editions PAC, 1975.
Robert Redford, Editions PAC, 1976.
Marlon Brando, Editions PAC, 1976 et 1979.
Steve McQueen, Editions PAC, 1978.
Le Film noir américain, Editions Henri Veyrier, 1979.
Le Cinéma policier français, Editions Henri Veyrier, 1981.

CLINT EASTWOOD

FRANÇOIS GUÉRIF

TRANSLATED FROM THE FRENCH
by LISA NESSELSON

ST. MARTIN'S PRESS / NEW YORK

Editor: Toni Lopopolo

Library of Congress Cataloging in Publication Data

Guérif, François.
    Clint Eastwood.

    1. Eastwood, Clint, 1930–   .   2. Moving-picture actors and actresses—United States—Biography.
I. Title.
PN2287.E37G83   1986   791.43′028′0924 [B]   85-25120
ISBN 0-312-14432-6 (pbk.)

First Edition

10 9 8 7 6 5 4 3 2 1

For Jacques Bral

Contents

Acknowledgments

The author wishes to thank Raymond Boyer, Jean-Pierre Busca, Luc Chomarat, Olivier Eyquem, Philippe Ferrari, Eric Leguèbe, Pascal Mérigeau, Alain Pelé, Jean-Pierre Vincent, Marie-Christine Fontaine, Michèle Darmon, and Warner-Columbia Films for the assistance and information they have provided.

He especially wants to also thank Clint Eastwood, for his friendly support.

072-605

Clint Eastwood:
The Good, the Bad
and the "Honkytonk Man"

"I'm afraid you've misjudged me."
—Harry Callahan in *Magnum Force*

In an Oklahoma field we see two farmers toiling with Grandpa and the kids. A duststorm is gathering force on the horizon. The clan makes a mad dash for the shelter of their run-down farmhouse as the air churns with reddish dust whipped up by an escalating wind. Out of the near blinding dust, an old automobile emerges. The driver falls out, sickly and dead drunk, is carried inside and put to bed. In the room next door lamplit faces lined by poverty and fatigue register chronic exhaustion. It's a scene reminiscent of John Ford's *The Grapes of Wrath*. The 1982 film *Honkytonk Man,* directed by and starring Clint Eastwood, opens in the early 1930s. It's a time Eastwood knows well, for he was born and raised in the wake of the Great Depression.

A Child of the Depression

Clinton Eastwood, Jr., was born May 31, 1930, in San Francisco. His father, Clinton senior, an accountant, worked when and where he could, dragging his family from town to town throughout northern California, the so-called land of opportunity. "Jobs were hard to come by in those days," explains Eastwood. "So there were times when we had to be separated; when times weren't good, I had to live with my grandmother, on her farm up near Sunol, near Livermore. We moved around so much—I must have gone to eight different grammar schools—that the family was about all you had. I didn't have a lot of friends; our family—my parents and my younger sister and I—was a unit. I think my parents and my grandmother—she was quite a person, very self-sufficient, lived by herself on a mountain—probably had more to do with my turning out the way I have than any educational process I may have gone through.

"They were very young parents—quite the antithesis of my own situation with my children. They were great parents. I was lucky to have them."[1] This constant uprooting made a lasting impact on young Eastwood. "I never had the time to make friends. Moving became a way of life. Basically, I was a drifter."[2] (The themes of constant wandering and of family unity up against the world at large figure prominently in two of Eastwood's key films, *Breezy* and *The Outlaw Josey Wales.*)

The sense of isolation brought about under the circumstances formed Eastwood's loner temperament, a brand of individualism which would deepen over the years. Clinton senior eventually found work with the Container Corporation of America in Oakland, California. Young Clinton enrolled at the local Technical High School where his height (6 feet 4 inches) landed him a choice spot on the basketball team. The budding athlete considered a career in professional sports and trained seriously while also working at odd jobs for pocket money. Eastwood played jazz piano and trumpet in a bar as well as serving as a lumberjack and firefighter for the Paradise County Department of Forestry. He graduated from high school in 1948. When his parents moved to Seattle, he chose to work as a lumberjack in Oregon, but the hard, lonely winters didn't suit him. He headed for Seattle to work in the blast furnaces of the Bethlehem Steel Company, determined "never to be dependent on anyone else."[2]

The following years were unremarkable. Eastwood served in the army, working as a swim instructor at Fort Ord, south of San Francisco, and was never called for active duty in the Korean War; he never really knew why he wasn't. At the barracks he got to know three young actors—Martin Milner, David Janssen, and Norman Bartold—and took an interest in their profession. Universal-International came to Fort Ord to shoot a few scenes for a film and an assistant director spotted Eastwood's remarkable physique. The director invited Eastwood to come see him at the studio when his army stint was over. Discharged in February 1953, Eastwood took the director up on his offer only to discover that the man in question no longer worked at Universal.

Eastwood decided to stick around and enrolled in business courses at Los Angeles City College under the G.I. Bill. Mornings he attended class, afternoons he worked as a gas station attendant, and evenings found him in the role of janitor at the building where he lived. He began dating Maggie Johnson, a model and swimwear designer, and they were married in 1954. Eastwood had kept in touch with his acting buddies from the army, who encouraged him to try his luck in show business—it was an iffy line of work but the studios were putting young hopefuls under contract. "A photographer, Irving Lasper, also pushed me in that direction. I signed a contract with Universal for $75 a week. It seemed like a fortune—my army benefits were only $110 a month."[1]

His screen test had been in the form of a filmed interview. Eastwood photographed well, but assumed his problems would begin when they asked him to *act*. The studio made its offer, he made his decision. With a salary guaranteed for forty weeks out of the coming year, Eastwood dropped out of college. For the next year and a half, frequently uncredited, often off-screen, he fed replies to the studio's stars—among them John Agar, George Nader, and Rock Hudson, in films such as *Revenge of the Creature* and *Tarantula* by Jack Arnold, *Never Say Goodbye* by Jerry Hopper, and *Away All Boats* by Joseph Pevney. These early performances proved to be a false start, however, and Eastwood ended up digging swimming pools in Beverly Hills to make ends meet before finding the security of a full-time role as one of the leads in the TV series *Rawhide*.

The "Good" Guy: Western Hero

Enter the first paradox of Eastwood's career: He attained stardom in a series that by virtue of its subject shouldn't have caught on at all. (In fact, *Rawhide* briefly stopped production after the tenth episode—but unexpected and overwhelming popularity assured its continued production and eventual longevity.) Here was a young actor with practically no track record taking on the role of an old-fashioned hero in the classic tradition: the noble cattle driver. Right from the start, despite himself, Eastwood inherited the sort of image first carved by John Wayne. (*Rawhide* was based on Howard Hawks's *Red River,* which starred Wayne.)

This image of unassailable integrity contrasted with that of Steve McQueen, for example, who, eight years earlier, had also had a celebrated television career playing a resolutely modern bounty hunter on *Wanted: Dead or Alive.* The classic angle was not displeasing to Eastwood. "I have to admit that I'm drawn to the style and spirit of the Western. I'm identified as a man from the West. And that's no accident. I've always lived out West. I've always liked the way of life, the code. And I like to go see Westerns."[3]

The Rowdy Yates character in *Rawhide* is without a doubt a "good guy"—a good-natured, smiling hero, loyal and true, bound to respect a code of honor as he takes on unmistakable bad guys. This was Eastwood's stock in trade, duly promoted by the CBS publicity department. If the Western hadn't been even more moribund at the movies than it was on TV, Eastwood might have stepped onto the big screen as the same sort of honest, hardworking guy.

But times had changed. A certain cynicism had invaded the Western and the public was growing more interested in enterprising mercenaries. Taking his cue from John Sturges's *The Magnificent Seven* (which was literally a "Westernization" of Akira Kurosawa's *The Seven Samurai*) a certain Sergio Leone was about to push Eastwood over to the bad guys, in accordance with no law aside from egoism and the profit motive. The result was an image considerably more profitable at the box office but ultimately more problematic for the actor.

The "Bad" Guy: Mercenary and Cop

Sergio Leone advised Eastwood to scruff up his image—let his beard grow, don an old poncho, and, so as to forever banish the specter of the clean-cut Rowdy Yates, always have a cigar butt parked between his lips. Eastwood, a nonsmoker, obeyed. He later explained that the cigars, which made him slightly ill, banished his stage fright and got him into the proper surly mood. The nameless hero of *For a Fistful of Dollars,* quickly nicknamed "Il Cigarillo," soon became more famous in Italy than Sophia Loren. The film was generally considered to be unsavory and its hero repugnant.

Leone would be judged differently from film to film and given serious consideration, but not so Eastwood, who became an all-purpose scapegoat for American cinema. After *Dirty Harry* and *High Plains Drifter* one could read outright inflammatory critiques in the press.

Because the object of this book is to retrace, film by film, the evolution of the Eastwood persona, and to follow critical response, in France as well as in America, to his screen portrayals, we won't go into too much depth here in the introduction. Since the image of Clint Eastwood as a dangerous actor-director (i.e. intriguing in his unsavoriness) has been widely perpetuated in the press, it seems worthwhile here to point out the major lines of attack to which Eastwood has been subjected over the years and to give him the opportunity for rebuttal through the eloquent device of the films themselves. And if this introduction and some of the film synopses take on a defensive tone, that is only to be expected in the face of detractors who seem eager to put Eastwood on trial. Many of the specific critical accusations have been mentioned in the film summaries which follow. (I direct those who wish further information to Jacques Zimmer's excellent article "Eastwood et la critique francaise" in *La Revue du Cinema,* no. 335, January 1979). For the purposes of this introduction, however, I should like to cite two lengthy articles published four years apart in two magazines representing the so-called "liberal" point of view.

Accusation number one: Clint Eastwood is the successor to John Wayne, which is despicable. French critic Michel Grisolia entitled his review of *The Eiger Sanction (Le Nouvel Observateur,* July 25, 1975) "A Child of John Wayne" and critic Pierre Murat cooly wrote (*Télérama,* October 31, 1979) "Will John Wayne's successor go even farther than the Duke on the road of racism and violence?" If Clint Eastwood is indeed the successor to John Wayne, cinematically speaking, then that in itself should stand him in good stead. Afterall, the Duke built a remarkable career, starring in at least a dozen classics directed by such masters as Ford, Walsh, and Hawks, among others, including *The Searchers* (which topped the list in a *Cahiers du Cinéma* survey of the greatest American talkies of all time) and *The Shootist,* an admirable conclusion to both a legend and a career.

Now, does all this have anything to do with the Eastwood persona? Is the latter at all similar to the image personified by Wayne? In *Rawhide,* yes, without a doubt—but certainly not in the films which followed. When did Wayne ever play a cynical mercenary, lawless and without faith? "I can shoot a guy in the back, but Wayne can't," says Eastwood. (Ironically, it's Wayne who was influenced by Eastwood in films such as *McQ* and *Brannigan.* In effect, it is Wayne's political opinions which are being singled out for comparison. But to the same extent that Wayne made known his political views and even made the promilitary *The Green Berets,* Eastwood has expressed his dislike for overt political commitment. When asked "How would you characterize yourself politically?" Eastwood replied, "I'm a political nothing. I mean, I hate to be categorized. I'm certainly not an extremist; the best thing you can say about extremists, either right or left, is that they're boring people. Not very flexible people. I suppose I'm a moderate, but I could be called a lot of things. On certain things I could be called very liberal; on others, very conservative."[1]

John Wayne considered Eastwood to be "the best cowboy in movies today." Poor Duke would be surprised indeed to see the interpretation his words have been given. This whole debate is even more amusing when one considers that Eastwood has repeatedly stated that he has only one idol—James Cagney—notwithstanding his special admiration for Marlon Brando's performance in *On the Waterfront.* (Eastwood has a certain amount in common with Cagney, who has complained of being "a dancer gone wrong," who built his career on portraying merciless killers and yet won the Oscar for his role in a musical comedy.) As Eastwood has explained countless times, "Maybe the thing that makes me work in the type of roles I'm more famous for, like the lone Westerner or the rebel police officer, is that I'm an individual in real life. . . . I think there's a dream in every man's mind of being an individual, but it's harder every year to be one. The tendency is to join something—join the left, join the right, join the Phi Beta this, the Kappa Gamma that. Everything is joining."[1]

Accusation number two: Eastwood is abominably macho. Michel Grisolia asserted that for Eastwood "all women are dangerous. If they're not lustful bitches or run-of-the-mill femmes fatales, then the poor girls have only to give in." Pierre Murat declared that "For Eastwood, a woman is always relegated somewhere between saintly virgin and whore." When these articles appeared, *Breezy* and *The Beguiled* had already been released, their content largely unremarked. Eastwood: "I'd hate to say I'm a pioneer with women's lib or whatever, but I think it's justifiable; it's probably been too long in coming. So many articles you read on it are absolutely boring and silly, but the basis for it is all there. I think women tend to be smarter than men in a lot of areas . . . you see a lot of terribly intelligent men with dumb women, but you never see terribly intelligent women with dumb guys."[1]

Accusation number three: Eastwood thinks he's Superman and asserts himself through violence. Michel Grisolia had this to say:

"When his eyes narrow it's to hold you in contempt; if you think he's listening to you, you're mistaken, and when he finally looks your way, you no longer exist. . . . He'll wipe you out with off-handed aplomb—and for this you should be grateful: Your death will be the gesture which saves America from the foul influence of foreigners." Pierre Murat shared his view: "Clint is a gentle diplodocus until a rascal treads on his paw, prompting his vengeance. This all goes to show that it's not easy to take over for that simpleton John Wayne, for whom everything was in its proper place—the good guys and the bad, the little woman behind the stove and the stranger out in the street. Everything Eastwood's done is nothing but a response, primarily through violence, to the evolution of a mentality which, according to him, can only lead to chaos." Eastwood's "response": "My films are tough films but there's a certain satire involved in the violence that I feel is a catharsis. I'm not a person who advocates violence in real life, and if I thought I'd made a film in which the violence inspired people to go out and commit more violence, I wouldn't make those films. . . . The basis for drama is conflict, you know, and physical conflict is certainly a very important part of it. You can't have movies and television with people just sitting around having arguments; no physical action, nothing to look at. You might as well tell the story on radio."[1]

The two critics did not shy away from gratuitous remarks to support their arguments. Michel Grisolia stated that "He has long since crushed those cigarillos from his Leone films under his Italian boot heel. Leone, who brought Eastwood's talents to light, was really only using him as a caricature." Leone put forth the opposite view in his appearance on a BBC special devoted to Eastwood. Pierre Murat glibly announced that "For more than ten years he has catalyzed the hatred of acid-penned liberals." False. Ultraliberal *Rolling Stone,* the home of "new journalism," has firmly defended Eastwood since as far back as *Dirty Harry.* Yet, in Michel Grisolia's view, "There is no one more antipathetic than Clint Eastwood."

In rebuttal, allow us to present the testimony of Arthur Knight, professor of cinema at the University of Southern California: "It's difficult to reconcile the real Clint Eastwood—gentle, soft-spoken, self-effacing—with the violent men he's played onscreen, men who were ready to shoot first and talk later, if at all. There are other contradictions; he's a physical fitness buff but a chain beer drinker; he enjoys shooting but refuses to hunt; hates giving out autographs, but the fans who besiege him whenever he makes a rare personal appearance are unlikely to discover this unless they become unbearably persistent. You won't find Eastwood in the 'with-it' spots of Hollywood; a big night out, for him, might be spent with a few friends in a bar. One with a good jukebox; he's a former musician who once played piano and jazz trumpet."[1]

Honkytonk: or Music Takes the Edge off Manners

Just like Bronco Billy under his circus tent, Eastwood claims to be, above all, a man who seeks to entertain. And entertainment consists of putting the interests of the man in the street up on the screen, dream and reality alike. "I'm deeply American in my attitudes and reactions," Eastwood explains. "Therefore I pay very close attention to my audience. My biggest responsibility is to provide what interests them, and my job is to make sure that my judgment coincides with what they want to see. Escapist entertainment is fine, but you also have to try to address any questions the audience may have."[3]

After the disappointing failure of *Honkytonk Man* it became obvious that what the public wants is a return to the strong hero in a rugged adventure, and Eastwood has obliged, to some extent, with the more recent *Sudden Impact* and *Pale Rider*. If Eastwood's film about the search for POWs missing in Laos ever sees the light of day, perhaps that will fit the bill as well. (In early February of 1983, the press made a great deal out of the mercenary commando raid financed by Eastwood in exchange for the right to adapt it to the screen. From there it was only one small step, a step blithely taken by one Jean-Luc Douin, to call Eastwood a "Reaganian mercenary."[4]) But the actor is finding it harder and harder to endorse this kind of personality, as the fallible, traumatized pilot in *Firefox* and the troubled police detective in *Tightrope* illustrate. Today the "friends" Eastwood would rather work with are musicians: Eddie Rabbitt, Charlie Rich, Mel Tillis, Ronnie Milsap, Merle Haggard, Glen Campbell, Jim Stafford, Johnny Duncan, Ray Charles, Fats Domino, Frizzell and West, Marty Robbins, Linda Hopkins, Ray Price—roving entertainers who sing of friendship, love, freedom, and the good things life has to offer. Through their music and the world of lovable misfits they conjure, Eastwood gets back to his roots and puts his heart on the line. "If ever I had a message to get across, you'll find it in *Bronco Billy*," Eastwood affirmed during the advertising campaign for *Firefox*. Make no mistake, Clint Eastwood has been "good" by necessity and "bad" by accident, but he remains "honky tonk" by choice.

1. *Playboy*, February 1974.
2. Stuart Kaminsky, *Clint Eastwood* (New York: New American Library, 1974).
3. Unpublished interview with Eric Leguèbe.
4. *Télérama*, February 1983.

The Early Eastwood

Revenge of the Creature

1955

Distribution: Universal-International
Producer: William Alland
Director: Jack Arnold
Screenplay: Martin Berkeley, based on a story by William Alland
Director of Photography: Charles S. Wellbourne (shot in 3-D)
Music: Joseph Gershenson
Length: 82 minutes

CAST:

John Agar: *Professor Clete Ferguson;* Lori Nelson: *Helen Dobson;* John Bromfield: *Joe Hayes;* Nestor Paiva: *Lucas;* Grandon Rhodes: *Jackson Foster;* Dave Willock: *Lou Gibson;* Clint Eastwood: *Jennings;* Robert B. Williams: *George Johnson;* Charles Crane: *the police captain*

The success of *The Creature from the Black Lagoon,* shot in 3-D in 1954 and directed by Jack Arnold, led to a sequel the following year. *Revenge of the Crea-ture* updated the story by transplanting the creature from its natural habitat to the Florida shores. After being captured, the "monster" escapes and spreads terror across a beach where the patrons of a nightclub have been dining in tranquility—which creates an effective contrast with the spectacular seizing of the heroine and the violence of the ensuing chase.

Eastwood appears in only one short scene. "I played a lab assistant who walked around with mice in my pocket or something like that," Eastwood laconically stated some time later. "I only had three or four lines and I can't remember a single word." The film is important all the same because it helped Eastwood get accustomed to the techniques making feature-length filmmaking. As Dewitt Bodden wrote (in *Focus on Film,* no. 9, Spring 1972): "The middle Fifties was a good time for an actor who wanted to learn about picture-making to be at Universal-International. The company annually made a whole series of very successful featurefilms, and Eastwood managed to appear in six of them where he received billing and footage. He played in others unbilled—voice off camera, the office worker who, back to the camera, opens a door to admit a star. But in *Revenge of the Creature* and *Tarantula,* he is in there helping hero John Agar battle giant monsters."

With Donald O'Connor and Richard Erdman in Francis in the Navy

With Maureen O'Hara and George Nader in Lady Godiva

Francis in the Navy

1955

Distribution: Universal-International
Producer: Stanley Rubin
Director: Arthur Lubin
Screenplay: Devery Freeman, based on the character, "Francis the Talking Mule," created by David Stern
Director of Photography: Carl Guthrie
Music: Joseph Gershenson
Editing: Milton Carruth, Ray Snyder
Length: 80 minutes

CAST:
Donald O'Connor: *Lieutenant Peter Stirling/Sliker Donovan;* Martha Hyer: *Betsy Donovan;* Richard Erdman: *Murph;* Jim Backus: *Commander Hutch;* Myrna Hansen: *Helen;* David Janssen: *Lieutenant Anders;* Clint Eastwood: *Jonesy;* Martin Milner: *Rick;* Paul Burke: *Tate;* Phil Garris: *Stover;* Chill Wills: the voice of Francis

Francis, the Army's "talking mule," showed up on screens in 1950 just in time to save Universal Studios from bankruptcy. This creation of David Stern (alias Peter Stirling) spoke snappy enough dialogue to win over a sophisticated public. The success was such that seven Francis films were made between 1950 and 1956. The first six were directed by Arthur Lubin, the last by Charles Lamont. *Francis in the Navy* figures next-to-last in the series and was the last to star Donald O'Connor. (Mickey Rooney took over the role in the final episode). Clint Eastwood was listed sixth in the credits and had several lines of dialogue. Critics took notice and found him "engaging," "handsome," and even "promising."

19

Lady Godiva

1955

Distribution: Universal-International
Producer: Robert Arthur
Director: Arthur Lubin
Screenplay: Oscar Brodney and Harry Ruskin, based on an idea by Oscar Brodney
Director of Photography: Carl Guthrie (Technicolor)
Music: Joseph Gershenson
Length: 88 minutes

CAST:
Maureen O'Hara: *Lady Godiva;* George Nader: *Lord Leofric;* Edward Franz: *King Edward;* Leslie Bradley: *Count Eustache;* Victor McLaglen: *Grimald;* Torin Thatcher: *Lord Godwin;* Rex Reason: *Harold;* Grant Withers: *Pendar;* Clint Eastwood: *a Saxon*

A pale rendition of the story of Lady Godiva of Coventry who, in the eleventh century during the Norman-Saxon conflict, agreed to ride naked on horseback through the town, a tribute exacted by her husband in lieu of levying a heavy tax on his subjects who had committed some serious transgression. Lady Godiva agreed to make this sacrifice only after having forbidden the town's inhabitants to appear in the streets or at their windows, upon pain of death. The only interest of this film is to remind us of the historical basis for the English expression *peeping tom* (the French equivalent of which is *voyeur,* one who views). In effect, a tailor, or perhaps a baker, was sufficiently reckless to spy upon the Lady covered only by her cascading hair, and would have paid for the opportunity with his life. The spectators (or "voyeurs," if you will) of this film, hoping to glimpse Maureen O'Hara in the nude, might well have done the same. As for Clint Eastwood, his name is listed last in the credits with the consolation of interpreting the role of "First Saxon."

Tarantula

1955

Distribution: Universal-International
Producer: William Alland
Director: Jack Arnold
Screenplay: Robert M. Fresco and Martin Berkeley, based on a story by Robert M. Fresco and Jack Arnold

Director of Photography: George Robinson
Music: Joseph Gershenson
Length: 80 minutes

CAST:
John Agar: *Matt Hastings;* Mara Corday: *Stephanie Clayton;* Leo G. Carroll: *Professor Deemer;* Nestor Paiva: *the sheriff;* Ross Elliott: *John Burch;* Raymond Bailey: *the old man;* Clint Eastwood: *the pilot*

So as to remedy the problem of world hunger, a scientist invents a formula which makes animals grow to gigantic proportions. The experiment goes awry when a giant spider escapes from the lab, terrorizing the populace and leaving destruction in its wake. At the end, said insect is bombarded with napalm. Our hero plays the pilot. Eastwood once again figures at the tail end of the credits. His lines are more than succinct and two-thirds of his face is hidden by his costume—the crash helmet and oxygen mask of a navy pilot.

Never Say Goodbye

1956

Distribution: Universal-International
Producer: Albert J. Cohen
Director: Jerry Hopper
Screenplay: Charles Hoffman, based on the scenario of *This Love of Ours* (1945) by Bruce Manning, John Klorer, and Leonard Lee, taken from the play *Come Prima Meglio di Prima* by Luigi Pirandello
Director of Photography: Maury Gertsman (Technicolor)
Music: Joseph Gershenson
Length: 96 minutes

CAST:

Rock Hudson: *Dr. Michael Parker;* Cornell Borchers: *Lisa;* George Sanders: *Victor;* Ray Collins: *Dr. Bailey;* David Janssen: *Dave;* Shelley Fabares: *Suzy Parker;* Clint Eastwood: *Will;* Gia Scala

Following a disagreement, a young doctor leaves his wife with their only child, a daughter, in tow. Years later the couple reconciles, but the child is unaware that it's her own mother who has returned. Thus, the mother must recapture her daughter's love. Based on Luigi Pirandello's play *Come Prima Meglio di Prima, Never Say Goodbye* is one of a series of Universal melodramas which made Rock Hudson a star. Douglas Sirk did preproduction work and brought over German actress Cornell Borchers to play the mother, but the film was eventually directed by Jerry Hopper, since Sirk was caught up in preparing *Written on the Wind.* Sirk, however, was called in during the shooting to finish the film. For the second time, Eastwood plays a lab assistant. The script graciously provides for a scene in which Eastwood appears with Hudson, but not in such a way as to be noticed. Universal neglected to renew his contract after this film.

The First Traveling Saleslady

1956

Distribution: RKO Radio
Producer-Director: Arthur Lubin
Assistant Director: Richard Mayberry
Screenplay: Devery Freeman and Stephen Longstreet
Director of Photography: William Snyder (Technicolor)
Music: Irving Gertz
Songs: "The First Traveling Saleslady" sung by the Lancers, "The Corset Can Do for a Lady" (music: Irving Getz; lyrics: Hal Levy)
Editing: Otto Ludwig
Sound: S. G. Haughton, Terry Kellum
Set Design: Albert S. D'Agostino
Set Decoration: Darrell Silvera
Costumes: Edward Stevenson
Hairdresser: Larry Germain
Makeup: Frank Westmore
Length: 88 minutes

CAST:

Ginger Rogers: *Rose Gilray;* Barry Nelson: *Charles Masters;* Carol Channing: *Molly Wade;* David Brian: *James Carter;* James Arness: *Joel Kingdom;* Clint Eastwood: *Jack Rice;* Robert Simon: *Cal;* Frank Wilcox; John Eldredge; Kate Drain Lawson; Lane Chandler; Clarence Muse; Dantel M. Wright; Harry Cheshire

With Carol Channing

Universal's failure to renew his contract reduced Eastwood to taking up shovel and pickaxe once again to dig swimming pools in wealthy Californians' backyards. Arthur Lubin, who had directed Eastwood in *Francis in the Navy* and *Lady Godiva,* came to his rescue and brought him to RKO where a "real" role awaited. In 1897, a corset manufacturer (Ginger Rogers) goes bankrupt after a Broadway show is closed down due to a musical number featuring her product. She heads out West accompanied by one of her models (Carol Channing, replete in "barbed wire" allure) whose attention is swayed by a young cavalry officer (Clint Eastwood).

Eastwood's image in this Western comedy is exactly the opposite of that which would eventually make his fame. Clean-shaven, hair slicked back, he is the "handsome cowboy," sufficiently rough yet endearing enough to appeal to a civilized woman from the East. This film featured the first close-up of Eastwood's career as well as more scenes with spoken dialogue than in all his films for Universal put together. Unfortunately, the distressing mediocrity of the overall acting led to commercial failure, confirming a decline in popularity for Ginger Rogers. Eastwood comes across as inconsistent, ill at ease, bordering on ridiculous. All the same the *Hollywood Reporter* (June 28, 1955) noted that "Clint Eastwood is very attractive as Carol Channing's beau."

Star in the Dust

1956

Distribution: Universal-International
Producer: Albert Zugsmith
Director: Charles Haas
Screenplay: Oscar Brodney, based on the novel *Lawman* by Lee Leighton (Western Writers of America prize, 1953)
Director of Photography: John L. Russell, Jr. (Technicolor)
Music: Frank Skinner
Length: 80 minutes

CAST:
John Agar: *Sheriff Bill Jordan;* Mamie Van Doren: *Ellen Ballard;* Richard Boone: *Sam Hall;* Leif Erickson: *George Ballard;* Coleen Gray: *Nellie Mason;* Paul Fix: *Mike MacNamara;* Harry Morgan: *Lew Hogan;* James Gleason: *Orval Jones;* Clint Eastwood: *ranch hand;* Randy Stuart; Henry Morgan; Stanley Andrews

A melodramatic Western in which the action takes place in the course of one day, between sunrise and sundown. A sheriff finds himself alone in his quest to see a professional killer hang for the murder of three farmers. After *The First Traveling Saleslady* this film is a return to basics which amounts to a regression, plain and simple. *Star in the Dust* has three things in common with *Revenge of the Creature,* Eastwood's

first film: It's a Universal picture, John Agar stars, and Clint Eastwood is not mentioned in the credits.

Escapade in Japan

1957

Distribution: RKO Radio
Producer-Director: Arthur Lubin
Screenplay: Winston Miller
Director of Photography: William Snyder (Technicolor/Technirama)

CAST:
Teresa Wright: *Mary Saunders;* Cameron Mitchell: *Dick Saunders;* Jon Provost: *Tony Saunders;* Roger Nakagawa: *Hiko;* Philip Ober: *Lieutenant Colonel Hargrave;* Kuniko Miyake: *Mitchiko;* Clint Eastwood: *Dumbo*

Young Tony leaves Manila by plane to join his parents in Tokyo. The plane is forced to splash down and Tony is rescued by a Japanese fisherman who has a son just his age. The two children get along fine and, taking the advice of an American pilot, decide to run away to look for Tony's parents. The pilot, named Dumbo, is portrayed by Clint Eastwood. This was his fourth film with Arthur Lubin and his second at RKO. Unfortunately, Howard Hughes had lost interest in the movies and, during the shooting, decided to sell the studio and all that went with it, including the film in progress, which would be distributed by Universal. This time around, Eastwood was discouraged. Only much later would he see the value of his unpromising debuts. "There were classes every day, and I went to them," Eastwood told Arthur Knight in *Playboy* (February 1974). "And I'd hang out on the sets, behind the scenery somewhere—trying to be very unobtrusive—and watch people operate. I think you learn from seeing a bad movie as much as you do from seeing a good movie. I once went to a film festival where the audience was made up of students— or I gathered they were—and I forget what the film was, but it wasn't very good. And all these kids were yelling, making noises at the film, sort of as if it were a Sunday matinee of five-year-olds. And that seemed kind of stupid to me. I thought to myself, 'Don't they realize this piece of crap on the screen can tell them a lot?' It's just like acting in a picture with a bad director; it gives you some point of reference, some comparison, so that when you meet someone who is halfway adequate, you see what makes the difference."

Ambush at Cimarron Pass

1958

Distribution: 20th Century–Fox
Producer: Herbert E. Mendelson
Director: Jodie Copelan
Screenplay: Richard G. Taylor and John K. Butler, based on a story by Robert A. Reeds and Robert W. Woods
Director of Photography: John M. Nickolaus, Jr. (Regalscope)

Music: Paul Sawtell and Bert Shefter
Editing: Carl L. Parson
Length: 73 minutes

CAST:
Scott Brady: *Sergeant Matt Blake;* Margia Dean: *Teresa;* Clint Eastwood: *Keith Williams;* Baynes Barron: *Corbin;* Irving Bacon: *Stanfield;* Frank Gerstle: *Sam Prescott;* Keith Richards: *Private Lasky;* Ken Mayor: *Corporal Schwitzer;* John Manier: *Private Zack;* William Vaughn: *Henry;* Dirk London: *Johnny Willows;* John Merrick: *Private Nathan;* Desmond Slattery: *Cobb*

With Keith Richards

23

Union Army Sergeant Matt Blake's mission is to escort a man called Corbin and his shipment of rifles which he intends to sell to the Apaches. Along the way, Blake meets up with Sam Prescott, a rancher and ex-Confederate Army officer who's driving his cattle to a distant railroad station. Despite their differences the two men strike up a friendship, to the considerable displeasure of Prescott's two associates: Keith Williams (Clint Eastwood), who has never accepted the South's defeat, and Stanfield. Apaches attack the group and steal its horses. The men are being picked off one by one, prompting Williams and Stanfield's decision to mutiny against Blake. Prescott is wounded during a skirmish, leaving Williams to take on Blake alone. Blake emerges victorious and Williams begins to see that Blake is courageous and his fellows are cowards. During an ambush at Cimarron Pass, Stanfield frees Corbin. But Corbin knifes Stanfield before being slaughtered by the Apaches with whom he had intended to take refuge. In the ensuing battle Blake recovers the stolen horses and, realizing that the heavy rifles will hold up their progress, orders the guns destroyed before hitting the trail once more.

Clint Eastwood was virtually the second lead in this 20th Century–Fox vehicle, but it remains, for him at least, perhaps the worst Western ever made and the "all-time low" of his career. That's a harsh judgment for a reasonably swift-moving effort directed by relative newcomer Jodie Copelan on an extremely limited budget. *Variety* on February 14, 1958, praised the direction (taking into account the low budget) adding that "Fine portrayals also come from Margia Dean, Frank Gerstle, Clint Eastwood and Dirk London." The film was rereleased in the sixties with Eastwood given top billing.

Lafayette Escadrille

1958

Distribution: Warner Bros.
Producer-Director: William A. Wellman
Screenplay: A. S. Fleischmann, based on an idea by William A. Wellman
Director of Photography: William Clothier
Music: Leonard Rosenman
Length: 96 minutes

CAST:

Tab Hunter: *Thad Walker;* Etchika Choureau: *Renée Beaulieu;* William Wellman, Jr.: *Bill Wellman;* Jody McCrea: *Tom Hitchcock;* Marcel Dalio: *Drillmaster;* Dennis Devine: *Red Scanlon;* Veola Vonn: *Madame Olga;* Clint Eastwood: *George Moseley;* David Janssen: *Duke Sinclaire;* Paul Fix: *U.S. General;* Will Hutchins: *Dave Putnam;* Tom Laughlin: *Arthur Bluthental;* Bob Hover; *Brett Halsey;* Henry Nakamura

An American makes his way to France during the First World War, joins the Foreign Legion, and ends up in the Lafayette Escadrille, soon to be famed for its armed daredevilry. Here Eastwood had the chance to work with Warner Bros. (the studio he would most represent as a star some fifteen years later), and, above all, with the noted director William Wellman who had already dealt with this subject matter in *Wings,* with Gary Cooper, the first film ever to receive the Best Picture Oscar. All the pieces seemed to be in place to insure success: the story (which was, in reality, based on Wellman's own experiences); the director himself, noted for his "men's films"; and the backing of an important studio. The result, however, did not live up to expectations, partly due to the performances Tab Hunter (a colorless actor on whose future a great deal had been banked), but also because the love story slowed down the film's rhythm. *Lafayette Escadrille* was both a critical and commercial flop and turned out to be Wellman's last film. In the role of George Moseley, World War I hero, Eastwood made his presence felt despite the scarcity of on-screen time called for in the script. He is not listed in the opening credits and has no dialogue. In retrospect, this taciturn aspect presaged his future roles; but at the time it was yet another frustrating part for a young actor who had seriously begun to doubt whether or not he belonged in the movies.

For country music fans, *Rawhide* is a melody by Dimitri Tiomkin (one of the most famous composers of soundtracks for Westerns) for a song performed by Frankie Laine, later covered by Johnny Cash and eventually parodied by the Blues Brothers in John Landis's film. But, *Rawhide* is also a pop culture landmark. This legendary TV series, 217 hour-long episodes, was broadcast on CBS every week from 1959 to 1966. For the purpose of our story, it is also the vehicle which "redeemed" Clint Eastwood and launched him once and for all on his acting career.

Let's back up a bit. One day, while paying a visit to his friend Sonia Chernus, who worked in the story department at CBS, Eastwood met Robert Sparks, executive producer in charge of programming. Eastwood recounted the meeting to USC film professor Arthur Knight as follows: "We were sitting there talking by this coffee wagon in the basement at CBS and this guy came up to me and said 'Are you an actor?' And I said, 'Yeah.' He said, 'What have you done?' So I listed a line of credits, always increasing the importance of the roles by about 50 percent, praying to God the guy would never ask to see *Ambush at Cimarron Pass.* Which, of course, he did. I was taking the whole thing kind of lightly, because, although I knew CBS was casting an hour television show, my agent had told me the lead had to be older than me—about 39 or 40. So the man—I didn't know who the hell he was—called me into an office and another guy came in wearing old clothes. Looked like he'd just been pushing a broom in the back room. I didn't know whether he was going to sweep under the chair or what."

The "guy" in question was none other than Charles Marquis Warren, who had started out in television some years earlier, producing and directing *Gunsmoke.* Warren had also left his mark in the annals of Westerns for having scripted the Gordon Douglas film *Only the Valiant* and directed a number of features including two of particular interest, *Arrowhead,* starring Charlton Heston and Jack Palance, and *The Black Whip,* featuring Angie Dickinson and Hugh Marlowe.

"So anyway, I was being very cool, and I just casually asked him, 'What's the lead like?' And he says, 'Well, there's two leads, and one is a young guy in his early 20's.' My agent wasn't bright enough to find that out." That very same afternoon Eastwood made a screen test, followed by another the next morning. "The big wheels at CBS liked it, and I was picked, and Eric Fleming was picked as the other lead. That was a great day in my life; the money looked to me as if I'd be in a league with Howard Hughes."

This promising new start too was almost cut short, however. After having shot ten episodes of a scheduled thirteen, production shut down. The reason: Hour-long shows were no longer marketable, and the public was already inundated by Westerns. Eastwood left Hollywood and went to visit his parents in Oakland. "On the way from Los Angeles to Oakland, I got a telegram saying that the series had sold, after all, and to be ready to work on such and such a day." Success would never again prove elusive, and in the seven years between the first episode, "Incident of the Tumbleweed Wagon," directed by Richard Whorf and telecast on January 9, 1959, and the last, "Crossing at White Feather," also directed by Whorf and broadcast January 4, 1966, Eastwood

would learn his craft down to the finest detail and appear in his first "spaghetti Western."

According to Stuart Kaminsky and Philippe Ferrari, *Rawhide* had two sources: *Traildriver's Diary* by George C. Duffield and the 1948 Howard Hawks film *Red River,* which in turn had been inspired by Borden Chase's novel *The Chisholm Trail.* The story is based on historical fact: the odyssey, around 1870, of small Texas ranchers driving their cattle north to the railroad, in Kansas. In the TV show, the ranchers have chosen the town of Sedalia as their destination. It goes without saying that various and sundry ups and downs befall them en route—and even today various chroniclers of TV lore are unable to remember whether or not they had finally reached their destination by the end of the 217th episode.

RAWHIDE

SEPTEMBER
NO. 1202

CLINT EASTWOOD

ERIC FLEMING

RAWHIDE

WHIPLASH

Gil Favor finds Jack Morse to be a changed man . . . wretched and miserable . . . blaming his plight on all trail herders.

Hoping to help Jack, and also save his own herd, Gil faces an angry man who thinks his whip is the only law of the range.

THE CAPTIVES

The strange actions of a pretty girl alert Rowdy that she and her father are being held as captives in their home.

When Rowdy tries to help them, he has to make his move with care in order to outwit three pitiless, villainous captors.

Various guest stars perked up the somewhat attenuated journey, enabling Clint Eastwood to play opposite Barbara Stanwyck, Mickey Rooney, Claude Rains, Walter Pidgeon, Cesar Romero, Vera Miles, Debra Paget, Elizabeth Montgomery, Dan Duryea, Julie London, Lon Chaney, Brian Donlevy, Neville Brand—in other words, Hollywood, both the old guard and the new. Not only did *Rawhide* enable the young actor to sharpen his skills as a performer, it sparked in him the urge to direct an episode himself. He planned one such show but at the last moment was unable to shoot it because higher-ups declared that episodes of other series directed by actors had been flops.

The role that made him famous would surprise his future detractors. Cast opposite head cattle driver Eric Fleming, Eastwood played a young cowhand, clean-shaven and good-natured to match, in a series devoid of sex and limited to "clean" violence. In this clear-cut world where the bad guys are unmistakable, Eastwood's part was straight out of the classical Western tradition established by Gary Cooper and John Wayne. He represented, without a trace of irony, the "good guy," the complete antithesis of the characters which would make his fame on the big screen. In certain episodes Eastwood, as Rowdy

Yates, came down with various diseases, was made a fool of by women, and ended up in fights which he couldn't hope to win. One time, he went so far as to get misty-eyed over a young lady. Eastwood is proud of *Rawhide* and its classic approach. "We did honest stories, pretty much the way they happened. Now and then we may have rearranged things to heighten the drama, but in general, we respected historical truth."

Ever since *The Man Who Shot Liberty Valance* we know that "when the legend sounds better than the truth, one prints the legend." Eastwood wanted to believe the legend and cultivated his image as a nice all-around guy, going so far as to offer the following advice in *TV Guide:* "Stay away from carbohydrates, especially rich desserts. Keep a scale in your bathroom. Proper rest, not noon to 4 A.M. Try to be optimistic. Eat fruits and raw vegetables. Take vitamins. Watch the amount of liquids you consume and skip beverages loaded with sugars. Avoid alcohol in excess." These telling details show just how carefully Eastwood cultivated the authenticity of his image (it would take him a good fifteen years to do

With Kim Hunter
("Incident of the Misplaced Indians")

away with the other image devised for him by Sergio Leone). But events would soon put an end to this admirable effort.

As early as July 1961 Eastwood complained about CBS policy in a *Hollywood Reporter* interview. "I haven't been allowed to accept a single feature or TV guesting offer since I started the series. Maybe they figure me as the sheepish, nice guy I portray in the series, but even a worm has to turn sometime. Believe me, I'm not bluffing—I'm prepared to go on suspension, which means I can't work here, but I've had offers of features in London and Rome that'll bring me more money in a year than the series has given me in three."

With Viveca Lindfors
("Incident of the Day of the Dead")

Eastwood had become a pro and well knew that an actor reaches a certain saturation point on TV. He'd set his sights on the big screen. Before *Rawhide* had run its course (the series finished in 1966 with Eastwood alone as star, Eric Fleming having been fired by CBS) he had agreed to take his chances in Spain, where he worked from February to June 1964 during a break in *Rawhide*'s production schedule. Ironically, the European foray would sweep away, in one fell swoop, the image he had worked so long and hard to create. Enter the macho cynic, lawless and without faith to boot—an image which would not be nearly so easy to shake.

With Doug Lambert
("Incident of Decision")

With Eric Fleming

The Rawhide Episodes

1 *Incident of the Tumbleweed Wagon*
D: Richard Whorf
Guest star: Terry Moore

2 *Incident at Alabaster Plain*
D: Richard Whorf
Guest star: Troy Donahue

3 *Incident with an Executioner*
D: Charles Marquis Warren
Guest star: Dan Duryea

4 *Incident of the Widowed Dove*
D: Ted Post

5 *Incident on the Edge of Madness*
D: Andrew McLaglen

6 *Incident of the Power and the Plow*
D: Andrew McLaglen
Guest star: Brian Donlevy

7 *Incident at Barker Springs*
D: Charles Marquis Warren
Guest star: June Lockhart

8 *Incident West of Lano*
D: Charles Marquis Warren

9 *Incident of the Town in Terror*
D: Ted Post
Guest star: Margaret O'Brien

10 *Incident of the Golden Calf*
D: Charles Marquis Warren
Guest star: MacDonald Carey

11 *Incident of the Coyote Weed*
D: Jesse Hibbs

12 *Incident of the Chubasco*
D: Buzz Kulik
Guest star: George Brent

13 *Incident of the Curious Street*
D: Ted Post
Guest star: Mercedes McCambridge

14 *Incident of the Dog Days*
D: George Sherman

15 *Incident of the Calico Gun*
D: Jesse Hibbs

16 *Incident of Fear in the Streets*
D: Andrew McLaglen

17 *Incident of the Misplaced Indians*
D: Jesse Hibbs
Guest star: Kim Hunter

18 *Incident Below the Brazos*
D: Jack Arnold
Guest star: Leslie Nielsen

19 *Incident of the Dry Drive*
D: Andrew McLaglen
Guest star: Victor Jory

20 *Incident of the Judas Trap*
D: Jesse Hibbs
Guest star: Nina Foch

21 *Incident in No Man's Land*
D: Jack Arnold
Guest star: Brian Keith

22 *Incident of the Burst of Evil*
D: George Sherman

23 *Incident of the Day of the Dead*
D: Stuart Heisler
Guest star: Viveca Lindfors

24 *Incident of the Roman Candles*
D: Stuart Heisler

25 *Incident at Dangerfield Dip*

26 *Incident of the Shambling Man*
D: Andrew McLaglen
Guest star: Victor McLaglen

27 *Incident at Jacob's Well*
D: Jack Arnold

28 *Incident of the Thirteenth Man*

29 *Incident at the Buffalo Smokehouse*
Guest star: Vera Miles

30 *Incident of the Haunted Hills*
D: Jesse Hibbs
Guest star: John Drew Barrymore

31 *Incident of the Stalking Death*
D: Harmon Jones
Guest star: Cesar Romero

32 *Incident of the Valley in Shadow*

33 *Incident of the Blue Fire*
Guest star: Skip Homeier

34 *Incident at Spanish Rock*
D: Harmon Jones
Guest star: Elena Verdugo

35 *Incident of the Druid Curse*
D: Jesse Hibbs

36 *Incident at Red River Station*
D: Gene Fowler Jr.
Guest star: James Dunn

37 *Incident of the Devil and his Due*
Guest star: Neville Brand

38 *Incident of the Wanted Painter*
Guest star: Arthur Franz

39 *Incident of the Tinkers Dam*
D: Gene Fowler, Jr.
Guest star: Regis Toomey

40 *Incident of the Night Horse*
D: Joe Kane

41 *Incident of the Sharpshooter*
D: Jesse Hibbs

42 *Incident of the Dust Flower*
D: Ted Post

43 *Incident at Sulphur Creek*

44 *Incident of the Champagne Bottles*
D: Joe Kane

45 *Incident of the Stargazer*

46 *Incident of the Dancing Death*
D: William Claxton, Joe Kane

47 *Incident of the Arana Sacar*

48 *Incident of the 100 Amulets*
D: Stuart Heisler

49 *Incident of the Deserter*

50 *Incident of the Murder Steer*
D: Joe Kane
Guest star: Jim Franciscus

51 *Incident of the Music Maker*
D: Bud Springsteen

52 *Incident of the Silent Web*
D: Joe Kane

53 *Incident of the Last Chance*
D: Ted Post

54 *Incident of the Garden of Eden*

55 *Incident at Rojo Canyon*
D: Ted Post
Guest star: Julie London

56 *Incident of the Challenge*

57 *Incident at Dragoon Crossing*
D: Ted Post
Guest star: Dan O'Herlihy

58 *Incident of the Night Visitor*
D: Bud Springsteen
Guest star: Dane Clark

59 *Incident of the Slavemaster*
D: Ted Post
Guest star: Peter Lorre

60 *Incident on the Road to Yesterday*
D: Bud Springsteen
Guest star: Frankie Laine

61 *Incident at Superstition Prairie*
D: Stuart Heisler

62 *Incident at Poco Tiempo*
D: Ted Post
Guest star: Agnes Moorehead

63 *Incident of the Captive*
D: Stuart Heisler
Guest star: Mercedes McCambridge

64 *Incident of the Buffalo Soldier*
D: Ted Post
Guest star: Woody Strode

65 *Incident of the Broken Sword*
D: Bud Springsteen
Guest star: E. G. Marshall

66 *Incident at the Top of the World*
D: Ted Post
Guest star: Robert Culp

67 *Incident of the Promised Land*
D: Ted Post
Guest star: Mary Astor

68 *Incident of the Big Blowout*
D: George Templeton

69 *Incident of the Fish out of Water*
D: Ted Post

70 *Incident on the Road Back*
D: Dick Templeton

71 *Incident of the New Start*
D: Justus Addiss
Guest star: John Dehner

72 *Incident of the Running Iron*
D: Harmon Jones

73 *Incident Near Gloomy River*
D: Bud Springsteen
Guest star: John Cassavetes

74 *Incident of the Boomerang*
D: Allen Reisner
Guest star: Patricia Medina

75 *Incident of his Brother's Keeper*
Guest star: Jack Lord

76 *Incident in the Middle of Nowhere*
D: Bud Springsteen

77 *Incident of the Phantom Bugler*
D: George Templeton
Guest star: Jock Mahoney

78 *Incident of the Lost Idol*
D: Ted Post
Guest star: Dan Duryea

79 *Incident of the Running Man*

80 *Incident of the Painted Lady*
D: Harmon Jones
Guest star: Mary Windsor

81 *Incident before Black Pass*
Guest star: Zachary Scott

82 *Incident of the Blackstorms*
D: Bud Springsteen
Guest star: Stephen McNally

83 *Incident of the Night on the Town*
D: Tony Leader

84 *Incident of the Wager on Payday*

85 *Incident at Rio Salado*
D: Ted Post
Guest star: Tom Tully

86 *Incident of the Sendoff*
D: George Templeton
Guest star: Darren McGavin

87 *Incident of the Long Shakedown*
D: Justus Addiss
Guest star: Skip Homeier

88 *Judgment at Hondo Seco*
D: Perry Lafferty
Guest star: Ralph Bellamy

89 *Incident of the Lost Tribe*
D: George Templeton

90 *Incident of the Inside Man*
D: George B. Templeton

91 *Incident of the Black Sheep*
D: Tony Leader
Guest star: Richard Basehart

92 *Incident of the Prairie Elephant*
D: Robert L. Friend

93 *Incident of the Little Fishes*
D: Justus Addiss
Guest star: Burgess Meredith

94 *Incident of the Long Count*
D: Jesse Hibbs

95 *Twenty-Five Santa Clauses*
D: Robert L. Friend
Guest star: Ed Wynn

96 *Incident of the Blue Spy*
D: Sobey Martin

97 *Incident of the Gentleman's
Gentleman*
D: Sobey Martin
Guest star: Brian Aherne

98 *The Captain's Wife*
D: Tay Garnett
Guest star: Barbara Stanwyck

99 *Boss's Daughters*
D: Sobey Martin

100 *The Peddler*
D: Laslo Benedek
Guest star: Shelley Berman

101 *Incident of the Woman Trap*
D: George Templeton
Guest star: Alan Hale

102 *Deserters' Patrol*
D: Andrew McLaglen

103 *The Greedy Town*
D: Murray Golden
Guest star: Mercedes McCambridge

104 *Grandma's Money*
D: Sobey Martin

105 *The Pitchwagon*
D: Marc Lawrence
Guest star: Buddy Ebsen

106 *Hostage Child*
D: Harmon Jones
Guest stars: Debra Paget, James
Coburn

107 *Gold Fever*
D: James P. Yarbrough

108 *The Child-Woman*
D: Murray Golden
Guest star: Cesar Romero

109 *The House of the Hunter*
D: Tay Garnett

110 *Reunion*
D: Sobey Martin
Guest star: Walter Pidgeon

111 *A Woman's Place*
D: Justus Addiss

112 *The Immigrants*
D: Tay Garnett

113 *The Devil and the Deep Blue*
D: George Templeton

114 *Incident of the Portrait*
D: Ted Post

115 *Incident of El Toro*
D: Thomas Carr

116 *Incident of the Hunter*
D: Thomas Carr

117 *Incident at Cactus Wells*
D: Christian Nyby
Guest star: Keenan Wynn

118 *Incident of the Prodigal Son*
D: Christian Nyby

119 *Incident of the Four Horsemen*
D: Thomas Carr

120 *Incident of the Lost Woman*
D: Thomas Carr

121 *Incident of the Dogfaces*
D: Don McDougall
Guest star: James Whitmore

122 *Incident of the Wolves*
D: Thomas Carr
Guest star: Dan Duryea

123 *Incident at Sugar Creek*
D: Christian Nyby

124 *Incident of the Reluctant
Bridegroom*
D: Don McDougall

125 *Incident of the Querencias*
D: Thomas Carr

126 *Incident at Quiriva*
D: Christian Nyby

127 *Incident of Decision*
D: Don McDougall

128 *Incident of the Buryin' Man*
D: Thomas Carr

129 *Incident of the Trail's Eno*
D: Don McDougall

130 *Incident at Spider Rock*
D: Thomas Carr
Guest star: Susan Oliver

131 *Incident of the Mountain Man*
D: Don McDougall
Guest star: Robert Middleton

132 *Incident at Crooked Hat*
D: Don McDougall
Guest star: James Gregory

133 *Incident of Judgment Day*
D: Thomas Carr
Guest star: Claude Rains

134 *Incident of the Gallows Tree*
D: Christian Nyby

135 *Incident of the Married Widow*
D: Thomas Carr

136 *Incident of the Pale Rider*
D: Christian Nyby

137 *Incident of the Comanchero*
D: Thomas Carr

138 *Incident of the Clown*
D: Don McDougall
Guest star: Eddie Bracken

139 *Incident of the Black Ace*
D: Thomas Carr
Guest star: Walter Slezak

140 *Incident of the Hostages*
D: Don McDougall

141 *Incident of White Eyes*
D: Christian Nyby
Guest star: Nehemiah Persoff

142 *Incident at Rio Doloroso*
D: Thomas Carr
Guest star: Cesar Romero

143 *Incident at Alkali Sink*
D: Don McDougall

144 *Abilene*
D: Tony Leader
Guest star: Audrey Totter

145 *Incident of the Red Wind*
D: Thomas Carr
Guest star: Neville Brand

With Ruta Lee and Eric Fleming
("Incident of the Reluctant Bridegroom")

With Gary Merrill and Eric Fleming
("Incident of Fear in the Street")

152 *Incident of the Rawhiders*
     D: Ted Post

153 *Incident of the Prophecy*
     D: Thomas Carr
     Guest stars: Dan Duryea, Warren
     Oates

154 *Incident at Confidence Creek*
     D: Harry Harris

155 *Incident of the Death Dancer*
     D: Thomas Carr
     Guest star: Forrest Tucker

156 *Incident of the Wild Deuces*
     D: Harry Harris

157 *Incident of the Geisha*
     D: Ted Post

158 *Incident at Ten Trees*
     D: Ted Post

159 *Incident of the Rusty Shotgun*
     D: Ted Post
     Guest star: Mary Windsor

160 *Incident of Midnight Cave*
     D: Thomas Carr

161 *Incident of the Dowry Dundee*
     D: Ted Post
     Guest star: Hazel Court

162 *Incident at Gila Flats*
     D: Thomas Carr

163 *Incident of the Pied Piper*
     D: Harry Harris
     Guest stars: Eddie Bracken, Everett
     Sloane

164 *Incident of the Swindler*
     D: Thomas Carr
     Guest star: John Dehner

165 *Incident of the Wanderer*
     D: Christian Nyby
     Guest star: Nehemiah Persoff

166 *Incident at Zebulon*
     D: Christian Nyby

167 *Incident at Hourglass*
     D: Christian Nyby
     Guest star: John Anderson

168 *Incident of the Odyssey*
     D: Thomas Carr
     Guest star: Mickey Rooney

169 *Incident of the Banker*
     D: Christian Nyby

170 *Incident at Deadhorse—Part I*
     D: Thomas Carr
     Guest stars: Burgess Meredith,
     Broderick Crawford

171 *Incident at Deadhorse—Part II*

172 *Incident of the Gilded Goddess*
     D: Christian Nyby

173 *Incident at Seven Fingers*
     D: Christian Nyby

174 *Incident of the Peyote Cup*
     D: Thomas Carr

175 *The Race*
     D: Vincent McEveety
     Guest star: Warren Oates

176 *The Enormous Fist*
     D: Bernard Kowalski
     Guest star: Lee Van Cleef

177 *Piney*
     D: Philip Leacock
     Guest star: Ed Begley

178 *The Lost Herd*
     D: Vincent McEveety

179 *The Backshooter*
     D: Herschel Dougherty
     Guest star: Louis Hayward

180 *A Man Called Mushy*
     D: Michael O'Herlihy

181 *Canliss*
     D: Jack Arnold
     Guest stars: Dean Martin, Ramon
     Novarro

182 *Damon's Road—Part I*
     D: Michael O'Herlihy
     Guest star: Fritz Weaver

183 *Damon's Road—Part II*

184 *Corporal Dasovik*
     D: Bernard Kowalski
     Guest stars: Nick Adams, John
     Barrymore, Jr.

185 *The Photographer*
     D: Vincent McEveety
     Guest star: Eddie Albert

186 *No Dogs or Drovers*
     D: Vincent McEveety

187 *Josh*
     D: Herschel Dougherty
     Guest star: Albert Dekker

188 *The Book*
     D: Bernard Kowalski
     Guest star: Pat Hingle

189 *Moment in the Sun*
     D: Bernard Girard

190 *The Meeting*
     D: Michael O'Herlihy

191 *A Time for Waiting*
     D: Charles Rondeau

192 *Texas Fever*
     D: Harmon Jones

193 *Blood Harvest*
     D: Justus Addiss
     Guest star: Steve Forrest

194 *The Violent Land*
     D: Harmon Jones

195 *The Winter Soldier*
     D: Justus Addiss
     Guest star: Robert Blake

196 *Prairie Fire*
     D: Jesse Hibbs

197 *The Retreat*
     D: Jim Goldstone
     Guest star: John Anderson

198 *The Empty Sleeve*
     D: Justus Addiss

199 *The Last Order*
     D: Robert L. Friend
     Guest star: Efrem Zimbalist, Jr.

200 *The Calf Women*
     D: Tony Leader
     Guest star: Julie Harris

201 *The Spanish Camp*
     D: Harmon Jones
     Guest star: John Ireland

202 *El Hombre Bravo*
     D: Philip Leacock
     Guest star: Frank Silvera

203 *The Gray Rock Hotel*
     D: Stuart Rosenberg
     Guest star: Lola Albright

204 *Mrs Harmon*
     D: Michael O'Herlihy

205 *Encounter at Boot Hill*
     D: Sutton Roley
     Guest star: Raymond St. Jacques

206 *Walk Into Terror*
     D: Thomas Carr

207 *Ride a Crooked Mile*
     D: Justus Addiss
     Guest star: John Drew Barrymore

208 *Six Weeks to Bent Fork*
     D: Thomas Carr
     Guest star: James Gregory

209 *Hostage for Hanging*
     D: Herman Hoffman
     Guest star: Mercedes McCambridge

210 *The Vasquez Woman*
     D: Bernard McEveety
     Guest star: Cesar Romero

211 *The Pursuit*
     D: Justus Addiss
     Guest star: Ralph Bellamy

212 *Escort to Doom*
     D: Alan Crosland
     Guest star: Rip Torn

213 *Clash at Broken Gulf*
     D: Chuck Haas

214 *Duel at Daybreak*
     D: Sutton Roley
     Guest star: Charles Bronson

215 *Brush War at Buford*
     D: Thomas Carr
     Guest star: Robert Middleton

216 *The Testing Post*
     D: Gerd Oswald
     Guest star: Dick Foran

217 *Crossing at White Feather*
     D: Richard Whorf
     Guest star: Albert Dekker

Eastwood:
The Legend

A Fistful of Dollars

1964 (U.S. release, 1967)

Distribution: United Artists
Producers: Jolly-Constantin-Ocean for United Artists; Arrigo Colombo and Giorgio Papi
Director: Sergio Leone
Screenplay: Sergio Leone and Duccio Tessari, based on *Yojimbo* (1961) by Akira Kurosawa and Ryuzo Kikushima
Director of Photography: Jack Dalmas and Massimo Dallamano (Technicolor/Techniscope)
Music: Ennio Morricone
Length: 95 minutes

CAST:

Clint Eastwood: *"The Man with No Name,"* Marianne Koch: *Marisol;* Gian Maria Volonte: *Ramon Rojo;* Wolfgang Lukschy: *John Baxter;* Sieghardt Rupp: *Esteban Rojo;* Antonio Prieto: *Benito Rojo;* José Calvo: *Silvanito;* Margherita Lozano: *Consuela Baxter;* Daniel Martin: *Julian;* Benny Reeves: *Rubio;* Richard Stuyvesant: *Chico;* Carol Brown

A stranger arrives in the town of San Miguel, near the Mexican border. While he freshens up at a well, two armed men strike another man and drag a child into a house. A little farther away a note pinned to a cadaver tersely relates the relative merits of staying home vs. going out. A man of the cloth tells the newcomer that San Miguel is a town of widows. Six or seven men appear and fire away at the ground around the stranger's mule. The stranger grabs onto the saloon's sign before being unseated from his perch. Silvanito, the saloon keeper, tells the stranger that only the undertaker is happy in San Miguel. Traffickers come down from Texas, cross the border and sell whiskey and guns to the Indians. What's more, the town is divided into two rival gangs, the Rojos and the Baxters. The newcomer inquires as to which of the clans is more powerful. "The Rojos," replies Silvanito. The stranger then provokes and kills the men who frightened his mule and who belong to the Baxter clan. He then offers his services to the Rojos. Their leader, Don Miguel, alerts him to the imminent passage of a cavalry troop and orders the stranger to lie low until his son, Ramon, returns.

In the middle of the night, Silvanito and the stranger observe what happens when an American troop encounters a group of Mexican soldiers escorting a stagecoach filled with gold. The Mexicans are cut down by machine-gun fire; the man at the trigger is Ramon. His men had killed the Americans and swiped their uniforms. The bodies are arranged in such a way as to make it look as if they'd fought among themselves. When the stranger is introduced to Ramon a short time later, Ramon announces that he has decided to make his peace with the Baxters and that they are to be his guests for dinner. During the festivities, Silvanito and the stranger take two of the dead soldiers to the cemetery and prop them up against the gravestones with guns in hand, so it looks as if they're wounded and waiting for help. When the Baxters return from dinner, the stranger tells them about the gold and also about the soldiers in the cemetery—in exchange for $500. He then goes to the Rojos and tells them that the Baxters are about to get hold of two soldiers who escaped the massacre and whose testimony would come in very handy in hanging Ramon. The stranger's fee once again amounts to $500. While the Rojos and the Baxters exchange powder-charged explanations at the cemetery, the stranger hunts for the gold and finds it hidden in a barrel. He hears footsteps. Overcoming the intruder, he discovers it's Marisol, a young woman whom Ramon loves and has been holding hostage.

The Rojos return from their expedition with Antonio, one of the Baxter sons. The stranger brings Marisol to the Baxters. An exchange of prisoners is scheduled for morning. During the exchange, the child whom we saw at the beginning runs toward Marisol. It's her son, and the man who had been beaten at the start is Julian, her husband. Ramon orders his men to kill Julian, but Silvanito and the stranger step in. Ramon yields and withdraws with the woman. During the night, the stranger helps Marisol to escape with Julian and their son. Ramon is waiting for him when the stranger returns. The stranger is tortured by Ramon's men but manages to escape after starting a fire. Driven mad with rage, Ramon thinks that the fugitive must be holed up with the Baxters and organizes a massacre of the entire family.

The stranger tends to his wounds in the shelter of

an abandoned mine and gets back into shooting shape. One day the undertaker comes to tell him that Ramon has captured Silvanito who was on his way to the mine with food. Hung by his thumbs from the sign of his saloon, Silvanito is being tortured when the stranger appears at the end of the street. A duel with Ramon is inevitable.

Eastwood had just begun his sixth season on *Rawhide* when a gap in production, from February to June 1964, enabled him to accept an offer which wasn't all that enticing at the outset. He was to star in a European Western—a German-Italian-Spanish coproduction to be shot in Spain by an Italian director whose script was based on a film classic which happened to be Japanese. Eastwood's agent had insisted that he be sent a script and Eastwood recognized a "westernization" of Akira Kurosawa's *Yojimbo*. The proposal didn't particularly interest Eastwood; even less so since he knew that the director had really wanted Lee Marvin or James Coburn but had been unable to afford them. Leone, having screened an episode of *Rawhide* at Cinecittà, fell back on Eastwood. The whole project didn't seem entirely serious, and yet Eastwood accepted. The official explanation, offered with Eastwood's characteristic humor, was that he took the job because it included a round-trip ticket to Europe. The real reason was because *A Fistful of*

With Pepe Calvo

42

Dollars came along at the perfect time to break out of his trademark public image.

"I was tired of playing the nice clean-cut cowboy in *Rawhide*," he told *Playboy*. "I wanted something earthier. Something different from the old-fashioned Western. You know: Hero rides in, very stalwart, with white hat, man's beating a horse, hero jumps off, punches man, schoolmarm walks down the street, sees this situation going on, slight conflict with schoolmarm, but not too much. You know schoolmarm and hero will be together in exactly ten more reels, if you care to sit around and wait, and you know man who beats horse will eventually get comeuppance from hero when this guy bushwhacks him in reel nine. But this film was different; it definitely had satiric overtones. The hero was an enigmatic figure, and that worked within the context of this picture."

The character was so enigmatic that he didn't even have a name. Fittingly, "The Man with No Name" became one of Eastwood's nicknames. He also didn't have (or practically didn't) any dialogue. "The dialogue was atrocious," says Eastwood. "It was an Italian's idea of American slang." This is just as

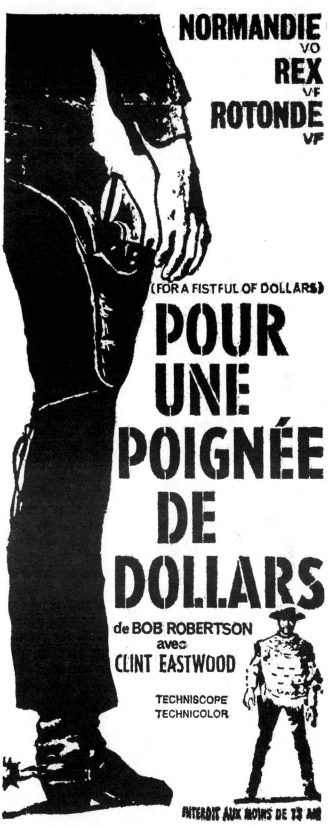

good an explanation as any, but it is more than likely a mere pretext. He would continue to pare down his dialogue as much as he could.

Eastwood created the character that would make him famous from A to Z. He also saw to his external presentation: "I went into Mattsons', a sport shop up on Hollywood Boulevard here, and bought some black Levis and bleached them out, roughed them up. The boots, spurs and gun belts I had from *Rawhide;* the hat I got at a wardrobe place in Santa Monica. The little black cigars I bought in Beverly Hills.'' The cigars would earn Eastwood another nickname, ''Il Cigarillo.'' A nonsmoker, Eastwood puffed on what he called ''pretty edgy cigars'' in his hotel room because ''they kept me in the right kind of humor . . . they put you in a sour frame of mind.''

Leone himself acknowledged that Eastwood made the character into even more of an antihero than the script originally made him out to be. The producers wanted a more ''expressive'' character, but Eastwood gave them a stubble-faced, taciturn ''hero'' sporting threadbare clothes and questionable standards of hygiene. Leone and Eastwood deliberately set out to create a baroque character in a baroque setting, made bigger than life and bent out of shape by satire. ''The film was obviously a satire,'' says Eastwood. But since Leone used close-ups to show what had always been omitted from American westerns due to censorship (''Leone did it because he didn't know about the Hays Code''), some critics took what was intended as ''fantasy'' at face value and described the vivid realism of what was absolutely unrealistic. ''Sergio and I got along fine,'' Eastwood told *Playboy*. ''Of course, at first we couldn't con-

verse much; he spoke absolutely no English, and my Italian was just *ciao* and *arrivederci*, and that was about it. So I did my own thing and he did his.''

Making *A Fistful of Dollars* proved difficult, and its ups and downs—lack of money, miserable shooting conditions—are well known today. The film's quasiclandestine release in a movie theater on the outskirts of Naples in the dead of August 1964 (a financial analyst had predicted that the film wouldn't bring in a cent) is also well known. The poster listed American-sounding pseudonyms. Leone was credited as ''Bob Robertson,'' Gian Maria Volonte was called ''John Welles'' and Marianne Koch got star billing although hers was only a bit part. And, of course, not a lira was spent on publicity. By virtue of some mysterious word-of-mouth miracle, *A Fistful of Dollars* left that suburb of Naples to conquer the world and beat out films like *My Fair Lady* and *Mary Poppins* at the European box office.

As for Eastwood, he became ''Il Cigarillo'' for the Italians, ''The fastest draw in the Italian Cinema'' for the Americans, ''El pistolero con ojos verdes'' to South Americans, and ''The Man with No Name'' in England. He had managed to make good on the wager he'd set himself as an actor: Make 'em forget *Rawhide*. But, without knowing it, he had also created a misunderstanding which hasn't been completely cleared up to this day.

For a Few Dollars More

1965 (U.S. release, 1967)

Distribution: United Artists
Producers: Gonzales-Constantin-PEA for United Artists; Alberto Grimaldi
Director: Sergio Leone
Screenplay: Luciano Vicenzoni and Sergio Leone, based on "Two Magnificent Rogues" by Fulvio Morzella and Sergio Leone
Director of Photography: Massimo Dallamano and Jack Dalmas (Technicolor/Techniscope)
Music: Ennio Morricone
Art Direction and Costumes: Carlo Simi
Editing: Giorgio Ferralonga and Eugenio Alabiso
Production Director: Ottavio Oppo
Length: 130 minutes

CAST:

Clint Eastwood: *"The Man with No Name"/Il Monco;* Lee Van Cleef: *Colonel Mortimer;* Gian Maria Volonte: *El Indio;* José Egger: *the old man;* Maria Krup: *the hotel director's wife;* Rosemarie Dexter: *Colonel Mortimer's sister;* Klaus Kinski: *the hunchback;* Mario Brega: *first man;* Aldo Sambrel: *second man;* Luigi Pistilli, Benito Stefanelli: *Indio's gang;* Roberto Camardiel; Luis Rodriguez; Panos Papadopoulos; Diana Rabito

Two bounty hunters, "The Man with No Name" and Colonel Mortimer, a former Confederate Army officer, are both on the trail of the same outlaw, a bank robber named Indio. The two men decide to join forces and to split the eventual reward. "The Man with No Name" wins his way into Indio's confidence by breaking one of his men out of prison and is therefore permitted to join the gang. Along with three other bandits, his first assignment is to create a diversion sufficiently large to enable Indio to rob a new bank. Eastwood summarily kills his three new associates, but returns too late to prevent the holdup. He lures Indio in the exact opposite direction from the appointed rendezvous with Mortimer. But the colonel, who was not born yesterday, has second-guessed the double-cross and is waiting for Eastwood at his "new" destination. The two men decide to make up and renew their partnership. They manage to convince Indio to help them steal a safe, then proceed to duck out with the gold. Indio captures them before they have a chance to hide the booty. After torturing "No Name" and the Colonel in vain, Indio lets them go in order to tail them to the treasure. A violent gun battle ensues during which our two heroes decimate Indio's band. The Colonel kills Indio, who had raped his beloved sister years before and in so doing hastened her death. Vengeance alone satisfies him.

"The Man with No Name," on the other hand, leaves town with a dozen cadavers piled up in his wagon, each good for a reward.

After the success of *A Fistful of Dollars,* Sergio Leone agreed to make not a sequel, but another film utilizing the same atmosphere, the same actors, and the same crew. There were, however, two important differences. The Jolly Company, which had produced the first film, dangled their fabulous profits in front of Leone but refused to hand over the director's share

FDM-25

unless he signed on for a second film. Leone refused, sued Jolly, and proceeded to produce *For a Few Dollars More* with his lawyer, Alberto Grimaldi, later to become one of the most important Italian producers (*Last Tango in Paris,* Fellini's *Casanova,* etc.) As a result, everybody revealed their true identity—the director signed his work "Sergio Leone" instead of the pseudonym "Bob Robertson," and Gian Maria Volonte was listed by his own name in the credits. As for Clint Eastwood, audiences no longer asked which European actor was hiding behind that name. The second major difference was in the budget: $600,000, or three times that of *A Fistful of Dollars.* Clint Eastwood received $50,000 for his role, as opposed to $15,000 for the preceding film.

These additional resources would permit Leone to expand upon several of his themes. "The Man with No Name" of the first film gained a partner, just as cynical on the surface, but in reality interested not in financial gain, but only in avenging his sister's death. Making him a former Confederate soldier served as an attempt to demystify the old South and to show, this time with a certain realism, that the end justifies the means. For this role Leone once more thought of Lee Marvin, but alas, Marvin had just signed to do *Cat Ballou.* Leone headed for Hollywood with a lingering memory of one of the killers from *High Noon* in mind. He screened the film and set off in search of Lee Van Cleef. "He's a Dutch Jew and I was immediately struck by his resemblance to Van Gogh," Leone would later say. "He carried the same brand of hopelessness, the hint of genius, the same intense eyes, eaglelike nose, the clear forehead." Van Cleef had not met with success as an actor and was living as a painter. Leone had a hard time convincing him that his acting offer was serious. Van Cleef finally accepted. For Leone, the presence of two American actors authenticated the background of his film.

For a Few Dollars More opens on a quote which would seem to indicate that the work to follow is indeed a sequel to *A Fistful of Dollars:* "Where life has no value, death sometimes has its price." But Leone clouds the issue in no time flat. Opposite the two bloodthirsty bounty hunters, Leone gives us an even badder baddie played by Gian Maria Volonte—and suddenly matters take on a new perspective. Van Cleef, the revenge seeker, becomes "the hero," whereas "The Man with No Name" is relegated to the post of "witness." The film abandons its satirical tone to rejoin the tradition of American Westerns. This second western shot in Spain would change nothing for Eastwood. His character still hadn't been given a name. And he seemed to be that much more cynical when contrasted with the positive motivations of his associate. The "good deeds" of which he was capable in *A Fistful of Dollars* (such as the rescue of the captured woman) were suddenly Van Cleef's domain, leaving Eastwood's character no humanizing traits aside from the lure of a reward and touches of offbeat humor.

The misunderstanding deepened. The film was judged to be morally repugnant. Leone, the director, was recognized for his undeniable qualities as an orchestrator of action; but the critics alleviated their uneasy consciences by redoubling their disdain for Eastwood, the actor. On a BBC program about Eastwood, Pauline Kael expressed the opinion that "One has no need of principles to kill," as if the actor himself were solely responsible for the films. From that point on, Eastwood was stuck with his image. Leone would try to modify the cumulative impression by casting Eastwood as the "good" guy in the next installment of what turned out to be a trilogy.

The Good, the Bad and the Ugly

1966 (U.S. release, 1967)

Distribution: United Artists
Producers: PEA for United Artists; Alberto Grimaldi
Director: Sergio Leone
Screenplay: Luciano Vicenzoni and Sergio Leone, based on a story by Age Scarpelli, Sergio Leone, and Luciano Vicenzoni
Director of Photography: Tonino Delli Colli (Technicolor/Techniscope)
Music: Ennio Morricone
Art Direction and Costumes: Carlo Simi
Editing: Nino Baragli and Eugenio Alabiso
Production Manager: Fernando Cinquini
Length: 161 minutes (English-language version; original length: 180 minutes

CAST:

Clint Eastwood: *Joe, the Good;* Eli Wallach: *Tuco, the Bad;* Lee Van Cleef: *Setenza, the Ugly;* Aldo Guiffre; Mario Brega; Luigi Pistilli; Claudio Scarchelli; Livio Lorenzon; Antonio Castale; Rada Rassimov; Enzo Petito; Sandro Scarchelli; Benito Stefanelli; Silvana Bacci; Antonio Casas; Aldo Sambrell

During the Civil War, Tuco, a Mexican bandit who's about to be hanged is saved from the gallows by a total stranger. It so happens that the stranger, whom Tuco dubs Joe, wishes to form a partnership. Two bounty hunters are hot on Tuco's trail. Joe's plan consists of handing Tuco over to the authorities, collecting the reward, and then saving Tuco from the hangman's rope at the last minute by cutting the cord with a well-placed rifle shot. This little ruse works several times in a row. But one day Joe abandons Tuco, leaving him to his unhappy fate. Tuco manages to escape, finds Joe, and forces him to cross a blazing desert on foot. Joe eventually collapses beside a stagecoach full of dead bodies. With his dying breath, the sole survivor manages to whisper to Joe the whereabouts of a hidden shipment of gold.

Tuco now has need of Joe to get his share of the loot, and their partnership is reestablished on a much-improved basis. Disguised in Confederate uniforms, they're captured by Union soldiers and sent to a prison camp directed by Setenza, a sadist who, it just so happens, is also in search of the hidden gold. Setenza tortures his prisoners in hopes of making them talk. When this fails, he suggests that they form a three-way partnership. The three men take advantage of the confusion created by the war to reach a cemetery where the gold is hidden in a grave. Once there, the three men draw their pistols to fight it out. Setenza is killed, whereas Tuco discovers that, thanks to Joe, his gun is suspiciously empty. Joe recovers the gold and leaves Tuco standing on a cross-shaped grave marker with a rope around his neck. Joe rides off with his share of the gold and, before disappearing altogether, fires a shot which, one last time, severs the cord that would otherwise hang Tuco.

The final installment in the trilogy, *The Good, the Bad, and the Ugly* synthesized the two preceding films, shed light on Leone's intentions, but left Eastwood's image unchanged. The actor began to feel the effects of this European period: "In the beginning I was just about alone; then there were two. And now there are three of us! I'm going to wind up in a detachment of cavalry," he declared just before shooting began. In effect, as Eastwood well understood, the only character who truly interested Leone in this $1,200,000 saga (with $250,000 as Eastwood's fee) was that portrayed by Eli Wallach. "He's the only character you really get to know," Eastwood remarked upon re-viewing the film. Leone, far from acknowledging Eastwood, finally realized his long-held dream of directing a real American "star." He couldn't get James Coburn or Lee Marvin for the first two, but he had Eli Wallach for the third and would go on to feature Henry Fonda in the next.

"Leone," critic Louis Seguin accurately pointed out (in *Positif,* no.95, May 1968) "gives the best part to the most foolish, most awkward, most devious, most fortunate, most greedy, most treacherous, in other words, the most human of his characters. Stuck next to a shaggy and belching Eli Wallach, slimy and splendid, granted a total freedom in which he luxuriates at every opportunity, gobbling up each shot with joyfully entertaining greed, Clint Eastwood and Lee Van Cleef come across as expressionless characters with poker faces."

This time the misunderstanding was thoroughly confirmed. Eastwood's range of expressiveness was equated with that of "a slab of boot leather." Overall, the American and European critical establishments acknowledged that the picture had a certain scope and praised the picturesque aspects of the mise-en-scène, but deplored the stereotypes incarnated by Eastwood and Van Cleef. From there it was only a small step for the critics to categorize the actors as being of extremely limited ability. With *The Good, the Bad, and the Ugly,* Leone finally escaped from the purgatory of underestimation as surely as he relegated his "discovery" to Hell. "The Man with No Name" had lost his novelty; the stereotype completely obscured his character. Upon his return to the United States, Eastwood tacked up on the wall of a friend's restaurant the poncho that had made him famous, never to retrieve it.

Happily (as is often the case), the public couldn't

Lee Van Cleef and Eli Wallach

have cared less about the critics' misgivings, and made the film into a huge hit. Ironically, the alternative press would be the first to support Eastwood. Richard Harmet, of the *Los Angeles Free Press*, wrote: "The Eastwood phenomenon is one of the more interesting things about American movies today. It started off with three Italian films—all directed by Sergio Leone as if the West were one giant opera stage—in which Eastwood played a scruffy, dirty, self-possessed Westerner, who didn't give a damn about anybody, and who was only vaguely on the side of the law.

"There was something about this part that Eastwood played so naturally that almost immediately made him one of our top box-office attractions. On the screen there seemed about him the absolute certainty that he stood above the rest of mankind, and that there was no one he couldn't take with his gun or his fists. Unconcerned about a higher moral order, he shot those who stood in his way.

"Above all, he was in complete control of his environment, certain of his actions and sure there was no obstacle he could not overcome and no human he could not dominate.

"And there is his appeal. Modern man—trampled on by government, beset by pollution, and manipulated by advertising—can only dream of control over his environment, and it is Eastwood who supplies that dream come to screen life.

"Eastwood has been shrewd in his choice of roles. He knows that no matter what the picture, whether it takes place during a modern war or on the plains of the West, his audience expects him to play the Man with No Name, someone who is rough, dirty, and in control."

Nevertheless, Eastwood became determined to demolish the very image that was being lauded. And in the meantime, *The Good, the Bad, and the Ugly* reinforced that same image at the box-office.

The Witches

1967

An anthology film made up of five unconnected stories by five different directors. The film has a total running time of 110 minutes. Episode number five, entitled "A Night Like Any Other," is 19 minutes long.
Distribution: United Artists
Producer: Dino De Laurentiis
Director: Vittorio De Sica
Screenplay: Cesare Zavattini, Fabio Carpi, and Enzio Muzil

Directors of Photography: Giuseppe Maccari and Giuseppe Rotunno (Technicolor)
Music: Piero Piccione and Ennio Morricone

CAST:
Sylvana Mangano: *Giovanna;* Clint Eastwood: *her husband;* Gianno Gori: Mandrake; Paolo Gozina: *Diabolik;* Angelo Santi: *Gordon;* Valentino Macchi: *man in stadium;* Armando Bottin; Piero Torrizi; Franco Moruzzi

Mario and Giovanna have been married for ten years. Giovanna, ever amorous, considers her husband to be negligent and inattentive toward her. She fantasizes situations in which she is forced to give in to Mario, whom she casts as a pitiless seducer. In the reality of home and kitchen, however, she has her hands full trying to spark even the most rudimentary interest on Mario's part, since he much prefers sleeping to the rigors of physical romance.

With Sylvana Mangano

Shot in the summer of 1965, after *For a Few Dollars More*, *The Witches* was designed as a vehicle for Sylvana Mangano, whose talents would be utilized by five great Italian filmmakers: Luchino Visconti, Mauro Bolognini, Pier Paolo Pasolini, Franco Rossi, and Vittorio De Sica. After having seen Leone's first two Westerns, De Sica publicly declared that Eastwood was "absolutely, the new Gary Cooper" and insisted on having him in *The Witches*. A risky bet, but a tempting one. Eastwood was then the most popular actor in Italy; adding his name to those of Alberto Sordi and Toto made good commercial sense. Unfortunately, Dino De Laurentiis's efforts to promote his wife Sylvana Mangano to superstardom rivaling that of Sophia Loren ended in failure, and

Vittorio De Sica was more or less considered a "has-been."

The film was badly received and Eastwood was pronounced boring and devoid of personality. "It was a parlor film, vacillating between dream and reality," Eastwood would later say. "Besides, it was nice to get out of my boots." Eastwood's role in *The Witches* remains of interest for two reasons. It marks the first time that he slicks back his hair, dons a suit, tie, and glasses, and tries his hand at comedy. And it's an unquestionable departure from the cynical, stubble-faced cowboy. To all appearances wild and virile, this American turns out to be a softie who prefers the pleasures of the hearth to the heat of passion.

Hang 'Em High

1968

Distribution: United Artists
Producer: United Artists/Malpaso; Leonard Freeman
Associate Producer: Irving Leonard
Director: Ted Post
Screenplay: Leonard Freeman and Mel Goldberg
Directors of Photography: Leonard South and Richard Kline (DeLuxe)
Music: Dominic Frontiere
Editing: Gene Fowler, Jr.
Production Manager: Robert Stambler
Art Director: John Goodman
Set Designer: Arthur Krams
Production Manager: Frank Mayer
Sound: Al Strasser, Jr.
Special Effects: George Swartz, Dewey Grigg
Length: 114 minutes

CAST:

Clint Eastwood: *Jed Cooper;* Inger Stevens: *Rachel;* Ed Begley: *Captain Wilson;* Pat Hingle: *Judge Adam Fenton;* Arlene Golonka: *Jennifer;* Charles McGraw; James Mac Arthur: *the priest;* L. Q. Jones; Alan Hale, Jr.; Dennis Hopper; Bruce Dern; Ben Johnson; Ruth White; James Westerfield; Bob Steele; Bert Freed; Tod Andrews; Michael O'Sullivan; Joseph Sirola; Russell Thorsen; Ned Romero; Jonathan Lippe; Rick Gates; Bruce Scott; Richard Guizon; Mark Lenard; Roy Glenn; Paul Sorenson; Richard Angarola; Larry Blake; Ted Thorpe; Robert Jones; Barry Cahill; John Wesley; Dennis Dengate; Bill Zuckert; Hal England; Robert B. Williams; Tony Di Milo

Jed Cooper is crossing the Rio Grande with his recently purchased herd of cattle when a band of vigilantes heads him off and accuses him of having killed a rancher and stolen the livestock. Before he knows it, Jed has been strung up on a tree and left for dead. He's rescued from death's door by a man who hands him over to the local magistrate, Judge Fenton. Recognized as innocent, Jed is set free and appointed deputy. He's to help clean up the territory and put a stop to the lynchings. The judge advises Jed to put aside any ideas he may have about personal revenge, but the scars around his neck obsess the new lawman. In the meantime Jed escorts a group of criminals to Fort Grant where they are sentenced and hanged. When the prisoners are brought in, Rachel, a local shopkeeper, looks them over carefully. Jed notices her, but chooses to relax with Jennifer, a prostitute, after delivering the condemned men to the gallows. One day, during an execution, Jed is shot and wounded by Wilson, the leader of the band of vigilantes that lynched him. Rachel nurses Jed back to health, during which time Jed discovers that Rachel is a widow. Her husband was murdered and she was raped by a man who remains at large. This explains her careful examination of every new batch of prisoners, in hopes of recognizing her assailant. Recovered, Jed heads out in search of Wilson. In the aftermath of a fierce battle Jed discovers that Wilson, preferring suicide to justice, has hung himself.

"Even with three films that were successful overseas, I had a rough time cracking the Hollywood scene," Eastwood told *Playboy* in 1974. "Not only was there a movie prejudice against television actors but there was a feeling that an American actor making an Italian movie was sort of taking a step backward."

The three films in question hit the U.S. in 1967, the producers of the first having finally decided to buy the rights to *Yojimbo* for countries outside Europe. Despite mixed reviews, the films immediately hit it big with the public. Nevertheless, Eastwood remained on the sidelines, settling for finishing up his commitment to *Rawhide* where, due to Eric Fleming's departure, he was now the main lead. Fortunately, Europe came to the rescue once again. French, German, Italian, and Spanish distributors were all clamoring for an American film starring Eastwood. "So finally I was offered a very modest film for United Artists—*Hang 'Em High*," Eastwood told *Playboy*. "It was a good film, analyzed capital punishment within a good story. I formed my own company, the Malpaso Company, and we got a piece of it."

The film itself might be modest, but Eastwood's salary rose to $40,000 plus 25 percent of the profits, which would seem to indicate that a major studio had at least a modicum of confidence in their new movie star. Aside from that, Eastwood's creation of Malpaso (Mexican for a bad pass or a false step, it is also the name of a creek which cuts across Eastwood's

property in Big Sur) demonstrated his desire to take charge of his career and not just settle for his newly won star status.

"My theory was that I could foul up my career just as well as somebody else could foul it up for me, so why not try it?" Eastwood told *Playboy*. "And I had this great urge to show the industry that it needs to be streamlined so it can make more films with smaller crews. The crews will be employed more, so there'll be just as much work. What's the point of spending so much money producing a movie that you can't break even on it? So at Malpaso, we don't have a staff of 26 and a fancy office. I've got a six-pack of beer under my arm, and a few pieces of paper, and a couple of pencils, and I'm in business."

The Malpaso Company (listed in the credits for *Hang 'em High*, but which would not be legally established until after *The Beguiled*) is still going strong and has employed the same four people for over fifteen years: Eastwood himself, Robert Daley (a former production accountant at Universal and now in charge of production), Sonia Chernus (in charge of scripts), and a secretary. Daley defines the company's goal as: "Put every cent up there on the

With Bruce Dern

screen." And so they do, by virtue of several guiding principles: Only start projects which can be brought in at a reasonable cost, shoot on location as much as possible, try to use the same crew to generate team spirit, take advantage of the latest technical developments (such as portable cameras). Eastwood has a reputation for remaining loyal to people he's worked well with in the past. Hence, he hired TV veteran Ted Post, who had directed several episodes of *Rawhide,* to direct *Hang 'em High.*

The film sets itself apart from the spaghetti westerns in that it takes place in a specific historical context: the era when, out West, a legal justice system replaced the somewhat more expedient process of lynching. This transition was not uniformly smooth, and public executions before the hymn-singing populace could be every bit as revolting as the lynchings

had been. But the "civilized" way had begun to spread and nothing could hold it back.

The raw, brutal violence of the film, coming straight out of the Italian westerns, was the only feature the European western passed on to its American counterpart. As for Eastwood, French writer Phillipe Ferrari points out: "His image is different from that in his Italian efforts. Physically speaking, he's clean-shaven and well dressed, sporting a wide-brimmed hat and an elegant thin cigar. Only the gunbelt is the same (and shall, incidentally, always remain so). As for morality, his motivation is no longer money, but revenge."

United Artists made back their investment in ten weeks, and to this day *Hang 'em High* remains one of their biggest-grossing films. Clint Eastwood had made a triumphant return and with this one film became one of the new stars of the American screen.

Coogan's Bluff

1968

Distribution: Universal
Producer: Universal/Malpaso; Don Siegel
Executive Producer: Richard Lyons
Associate Producer: Irving Leonard
Director: Don Siegel
Assistant Director: Joe Cavalier
Screenplay: Herman Miller, Dean Riesner, and Howard Rodman, based on a story by Herman Miller
Director of Photography: Bud Thackery (Technicolor)
Music: Lalo Schifrin
Editing: Sam Waxman
Dialogue Coach: Scott Hale
Art Directors: Alexander Golitzen and Robert C. MacKichan
Set Design: John MacCarthy and John Austin
Costumes: Helen Colvig
Length: 94 minutes

CAST:

Clint Eastwood: *Coogan;* Lee J. Cobb: *Detective McElroy;* Susan Clark: *Julie;* Tisha Sterling: *Linny* Raven; Don Stroud: *Ringerman;* Betty Field: *Mrs. Ringerman;* Tom Tully: *MacCrea;* Melodie Johnson: *Millie;* James Edwards: *Jackson;* Rudy Diaz: *Running Bear;* David F. Doyle: *Pushie;* Louis Zorich: *taxi driver;* James Gavin: *Ferguson;* Meg Myles: *Big Red;* Seymour Cassel: *young hood;* Marjorie Bennett: *Mrs. Fowler;* John Coe: *bellboy;* Skip Battyn: *Omega;* Albert Popwell: *Wonderful Digby;* James MacCallion; Syl Lamont; Jess Osuna; Jerry Summers; Antonia Rey; Marya Henriques; Conrad Bain: *man on Madison Avenue;* Albert Henderson

The New York police have just apprehended a young man named James Ringerman, wanted for murder in Arizona, and Walt Coogan, assistant sheriff in Piute County, Arizona, is sent to New York to extradite him. When Coogan arrives, Detective Lieutenant McElroy informs him that Ringerman has been hospitalized for an overdose of LSD. Obliged to extend his stay, Coogan gets to know Julie Roth, a probation officer. Impatient, Coogan bluffs his way past hospital personnel and takes charge of his prisoner, but not before Ringerman has a chance to whisper something to the young woman visiting him, Linny Raven. At the heliport Coogan is attacked and knocked out by Ringerman's accomplices. Seriously hurt, Coogan is hospitalized. McElroy informs him that the affair has

been taken out of his hands. To help him calm down, Julie invites Coogan to her place. There, Coogan discovers that Linny is one of Julie's "clients." He writes down Linny's address and pays her a visit. Linny allows Coogan to seduce her and promises to lead him to Ringerman. She takes him to a pool hall where Ringerman's friends lie in wait, and slips away. Coogan emerges not entirely uninjured from the resulting fight. He returns to Linny's place and beats her savagely until she agrees to take him to Ringerman's real hideout at Fort Tryon Park. Ringerman makes a run for it and Coogan goes tearing after him on a motorcycle.

For his return to Universal, the studio where he'd made his screen debut, Eastwood, now an actor of note, found himself presented with a script only three-fourths completed. "*Coogan's Bluff* started out as a story, not a complete story, but I thought it had potential so I signed a deal with Universal to develop it. It was assigned to a guy named Alex Segal, who just won an Emmy, I believe, for doing *Death of a Salesman*. He and another writer sat down, we had a meeting and put some pretty good work in on it, but we got to a certain point and we were stymied. They didn't know where to go with the character—I never did find out the full details. We had a limited time in which to shoot the damn thing—and the agency and the studio said, 'You've got to find another director.'"[1]

Coogan's Bluff was, in effect, the first film put into production by Malpaso and it was up to Eastwood to choose a director. Richard Lyons, a producer and screenwriter at the studio, suggested Don Siegel. Eastwood screened Siegel's work and was favorably impressed by *Stranger on the Run* and *The Killers;* Siegel, when approached, wished in turn to see the Leone trilogy. He found Eastwood to his liking and accepted the project. "*Coogan's Bluff* was born out of chaos," Siegel would later say. "I came on the picture in 1968, after five scripts had been written and one director had quit."[2]

All difficulties were far from being resolved, however. Siegel discovered that Eastwood had very distinct ideas about the character he was to play when Eastwood turned down a new version of the script and began to contemplate abandoning the project altogether. Finally, after the ninth rewrite, the two men joined forces, decided to string together all the scenes they liked from all the preceding versions, and hired Dean Riesner, screenwriter for *Stranger on the Run,* to polish it into a cohesive whole. In the meantime, Eastwood had radically modified the Coogan character: "Originally they were playing the guy as much more of a bumbling type. . . . The writer working with the first director saw the guy as a guy who's always losing his wallet and being taken by all the people in the big city. Well, I thought that had been done a lot in the past, with James Stewart and a lot of

guys. I felt, what happened if it doesn't mean anything that he's a small-town guy? Maybe he was in the war in Korea, he's traveled a little bit around the world, and he's been exposed to other things—just because he's not a New Yorker doesn't mean he's a clod. Plus the fact that his kind of prairie cunning might work well for him against a big city background. We got together, hashed it out and Siegel liked that idea. I liked some of his ideas, we kicked it around and came to a meeting of the minds."[1]

At the start of the film Coogan arrests an Indian chief who has escaped from the reservation, refuses to offer him a cigarette, and leaves him handcuffed while paying his "respects" to a lady friend. Then Coogan arrives in New York and, Stetson in place,

looks out over the city from atop a bridge thinking how glorious all this must have been before civilization turned it rotten. Critics tossed off Coogan as another typical Eastwood brute and stopped there, neglecting to acknowledge that Coogan evolves a great deal in the course of the film. First of all, his behavior, if not altogether justified, is at least explained: He feels responsible for a prisoner whose death came about through negligence. Coogan's confrontation with the old cop, played by Lee J. Cobb, and the various pitfalls of the city teach him an essential lesson: The drugged-out criminal he's after is a product of the city just as the Indian chief was the product of living conditions on the reservation. In the final analysis, if the urban cop recognizes the stubborn courage of the "country bumpkin," the bumpkin makes his symbolic concession to "civilization" by offering his prisoner the cigarette he had refused the Indian at the start. Coogan has not buckled under ridicule or questioned his own basic moral principles, but he has become a bit more humane and open-minded.

As usual, Eastwood left most of the dialogue to his co-stars—here, Lee J. Cobb. He says little and devotes himself to the action, which was as good a way as any to maintain the basic misunderstanding about Eastwood's work. Siegel understood perfectly and explained: "I found that he's inclined to underestimate himself a little as an actor, in terms of the range

he can cover. . . . Clint's character is far from mundane or ordinary. He is a tarnished super hero, actually an anti-hero. You can poke at a character like that. He makes mistakes, does things in questionable taste, is vulnerable. He's not a white knight rescuing the girl; he seduces her."[2]

Coogan's Bluff reconfirmed Eastwood's popularity at the American box office and inspired the TV series *McCloud,* starring Dennis Weaver as a country sheriff in the big city.

1. Patrick MacGilligan, "Interview With Clint Eastwood," *Focus on Film,* no. 25, Summer-Fall 1976.
2. Alan Lovell, *Don Siegel,* (London: British Film Institute, 1975).

Where Eagles Dare

1969

Distribution: MGM
Producers: MGM/Winkast; Elliott Kastner
Associate Producers: Denis Holt and Richard McWhorter
Director: Brian G. Hutton
Second Unit Director: Yakima Canutt
Screenplay: Alistair MacLean
Dialogue coach: Alfredo Lettieri
Director of photography: Arthur Ibbetson (Metrocolor/Panavision, 70-mm)
Music: composed and directed by Ron Goodwin
Editing: John Jympson (picture); Jonathan Bates (sound)
Art Director: Peter Mullins
Length: 158 minutes

CAST:

Richard Burton: *John Smith;* Clint Eastwood: *Lieutenant Morris Schaffer;* Mary Ure: *Mary Ellison;* Patrick Wymark: *Wyatt Turner;* Michael Hordern: *Vice-Admiral Rolland;* Donald Houston: *Olaf Christiansen;* Peter Barkworth: *Berkeley;* Ferdy Mayne: *German officer;* Neil MacCarthy: *Torrance-Smythe;* William Squire: *Lee Thomas;* Brook Williams: *Sergeant Harrod;* Ingrid Pitt: *Heidi;* Robert Beatty: *Cartwright-Jones;* Anton Diffring: *Colonel Kramer*

An English commando unit headed by Commander John Smith is to rescue an American general, held prisoner by the Germans in a fort on a peak in the Bavarian Alps, before he is tortured into revealing the plans for the Allied landings in Europe. Smith is assisted by an American ranger, Lieutenant Morris Schaffer. The commando unit parachutes into enemy territory. One of its members is found dead and Smith suspects the presence of a double agent in their ranks. While the men rest up, Smith meets with Mary Ellison at the village inn. Mary is to help them penetrate the fortress by being hired, along with a friend, as a servant girl. The stronghold can only be approached via aerial cable car. Having narrowly escaped a blast at the inn, Smith and Schaffer manage to penetrate the stronghold with Mary's help and get as far as the American general who reveals himself to be nothing more than an actor who has been hired to help smoke out a network of traitors who have infiltrated the British Secret Service. Smith introduces himself as a double agent and disarms Schaffer. Then, when the traitors in his squad have been revealed, he turns the situation around by taking them prisoner before the flabbergasted German High Command. Smith, Schaffer, and the prisoners escape from the château by cable car, which marks the debut of an insane chase which continues right onto the aircraft heading back to England with the escaped commandos. Only on board the plane does Smith reveal the identity of the head of the spy network that has infiltrated the British Secret Service.

If one is to believe Richard Burton, *Where Eagles Dare* came about because his sons, disappointed by their father's career in "complicated" and "intellectual" films, wanted to see him play a "real hero." And of course, since Burton's career was beginning to lose steam, a superproduction aimed at the general public couldn't help but boost his status as in international star. Burton asked his friend Elliott Kastner to find a suitable vehicle. Kastner contacted Alistair MacLean, whose best-selling novels (*The Guns of Navarone,* among others) had been the basis for several blockbuster movies. MacLean had nothing on hand. Kastner suggested that the author switch his usual method around by writing a scenario first which he might *then* turn into a novel. MacLean accomplished the task in six weeks and a major film was underway.

To inject a little new blood into the project, Kastner hired Brian G. Hutton, a young director with only three films to his credit: *Wild Seed, The Pad and How to Use It,* and a detective story called *Sol Madrid.* Shooting took place in Austria and made use of the Schloss Hohenwerfen, the famous Bavarian castle which dates from the eleventh century. When location scouts appropriated it, it was serving as a police academy. The film proved to be one of the most rigorous shoots in MGM's history. The equipment had to be transported to the castle, situated on a mountain peak, via a perilous road in the dead of winter. The temperature dipped below zero, the risk of avalanche was ever-present, and an assortment of blizzards and other storms didn't make things any easier for the crew. What's more, the script called for plenty of action scenes—a fight on the roof of a suspended cable car, tricky climbs, explosions—which were assigned to Yakima Canutt, the man behind the famous chariot race in *Ben-Hur.* The stuntmen took enormous risks, which led Eastwood to remark that the film should have been called *Where Doubles Dare.*

Where Eagles Dare is a significant film for Eastwood. Second billing in a superproduction with the likes of Burton, an actor who commanded international acclaim as one of the most gifted performers of his time, was not a bad place to be. Eastwood's fee was $800,000; Burton received $1,200,000.

The film measures up to its ambitions. It succeeds at maintaining a breathless pace and an epic visual scope for two hours and forty minutes, and remains today one of the best adventure films of the sixties. It is an "adventure" as opposed to a "war" film *Where*

Eagles Dare only appears to be a war film. The war is little more than a backdrop—and, unlike characters in true war films, the characters here are only slightly concerned with the moral or political implications of their actions. There are plenty of twists in the story integrated into a skillful blend of spectacular scenes taut with police-thriller suspense. As the French journalist Roland Lacourbe pointed out in 1982, "*Where Eagles Dare* foreshadowed, by a good dozen years, the 'return to adventure' for which we credit *Raiders of the Lost Ark*."[1]

The character of the American ranger is typically Eastwoodian. Hutton said, "He is revealed to be a professional assassin, the legitimate heir to No Name." This comment provides a key to the character, suggest critics David Downing and Gary Herman. "Unlike Newman, McQueen, or Nicholson, audiences do not see Eastwood's characters as an extension of himself. On the contrary, like Bogart, Cagney and Gary Cooper, they see him as an extension of his characters. You don't identify with Eastwood, you emulate him or desire him. This means that the perceptive filmmaker will cast Eastwood in a role which confirms the qualities his other characters display. He does not have the flexibility of a number of his contemporaries, who, finding themselves in an unlikely cinematic situation, can carry off the portrayal simply by seeming to be themselves. Siegel suggests that Eastwood underestimates his range as an actor, but experience has shown that some parts he undertakes are measurably less successful than others."[2]

This analysis is relatively accurate, except insofar as it attributes modifications in the character to the director, Hutton, which are due entirely to the actor himself. At the time Eastwood underestimated his abilities and preferred to play on the side of caution. "When they gave me the script," he remarked in 1977, "I had an enormous amount of dialogue. I told the director: Burton has a magnificent voice. Let him do the talking, I'll do the killing."[3] Richard Burton joined Siegel in his opinion that, "If Eastwood's acting is lethargic, then it's a dynamic lethargy. He's descended from the same line as Tracy, Mitchum and Stewart—one of those actors who appear to do nothing, but do everything. The misunderstanding stems from the fact that he reduces his dialogue to an absolute minimum. If he's got four lines to deliver, he says four words."[3]

---

1. *Télé-Ciné-Video*, no. 24, December 1982.
2. *Clint Eastwood, All American Anti-Hero* (Omnibus Press, 1977).
3. "The Man with No Name" (television broadcast), BBC, February 23, 1977.

With Ingrid Pitt, Mary Ure, and Richard Burton

Paint Your Wagon

1969

Distribution: Paramount
Producers: Paramount/Malpaso; Alan Jay Lerner
Associate Producer: Tom Shaw
Production Coordinator: Gene Levy
Production Assistants: Jonas Halperin and Joseph J. Lilley
Director: Joshua Logan
Assistant Director: Jack Roe
First Assistant on Second Unit: Al Murphy
Second Unit Directors: Tom Shaw and Fred Lemoine
Screenplay and Musical Numbers: Alan Jay Lerner, adapted by Paddy Chayefsky, based on the musical comedy *Paint Your Wagon* by A. J. Lerner and Frederick Loewe, presented on the stage by Cheryl Crawford. Screenplay supervised by Marshall Wolins
Dialogue coach: Joseph Curtis
Director of Photography: William A. Fraker (Technicolor/Panavision, 70-mm)
Second Unit Photography: Loyal Griggs
Aerial Photography: Nelson Tyler
Music: Frederick Loewe
Credit Sequence: David Stone Martin
Orchestral Music Scored and Conducted by: Nelson Riddle

Choral Arrangements and Music: Joseph J. Lilley
Choral Music Conducted by: Roger Wagner
Music for Additional Songs by: André Previn
Art Director: Carl Braunger
Costumes and Production Design: John Truscott
Costume Supervisor: Bill Jobe
Costume Coordinator: Anne Laune
Makeup: Frank McCoy
Hairdresser: Vivian Zavitz
Set decorator: James I. Berkey
Special Effects: Maurice Ayres and Larry Hampton
Camera Operator: David Walsh
Camera Assistant: Bob Byrne
Sound Mixer: William Randall
Stereophonic Rerecording Supervisor: Fred Hynes
Choreography: ''Gold Fever'' and ''Best Thing'': Jack Baker
Gaffer: Joe Smith
Key Grip: Tom May
Property Master: Tom Eaton
Length: 169 minutes

CAST:

Lee Marvin: *Ben Rumson;* Clint Eastwood: *Pardner;* Jean Seberg: *Elizabeth;* Harve Presnell: *Rotten Luck Willie;* Ray Walston: *''Mad Jack'' Duncan;* Tom Ligon: *Horton MacFenty;* Alan Dexter: *Parson;* Wil-

With Jean Seberg and Lee Marvin

liam O'Connell: *Horace Tabor;* Ben Baker: *Haywood Holbrook;* Alan Baxter: *Mr. MacFenty;* Paula Trueman: *Mrs. MacFenty;* Robert Easton: *Atwell;* Geoffrey Norman: *Foster;* H. B. Haggerty: *Steve Bull;* Terry Jenkins: *Joe Mooney;* Karl Bruck: *Shermerhorn;* John Mitchum: *Jacob Woodling;* Sue Casey: *Sarah Woodling;* Eddie Little Sky: *Indian;* Harvey Parry: *Higgins;* H. W. Gim: *Wong;* William Mims: *a man;* Roy Jenson: *Hennessey;* Pat Hawley: *Clendennon*

During the Gold Rush days of California, Ben Rumson, an old prospector prone toward fighting and drunkeness, saves the life of Pardner, a gentle and peaceful young farmer. The two men become friends and partners. Rumson can't take the bachelor life and buys a wife from a Mormon who has one to spare. The presence of the newcomer, Elizabeth, spreads trouble in the prospecting community. As a result, Rumson heads off on a mission to fetch a wagonload of prostitutes and proceeds to install them in headquarters at the Grizzly Bear Saloon. While he's gone, Pardner and Elizabeth discover they love each other. Rumson hears the bad news and wishes to break with his friend. But Elizabeth steps in. If a Mormon can have two wives, what then should prevent a woman from having two husbands? A ménage à trois is set up on a trial basis. All goes well until the day the trio rescues the MacFenty family from a blizzard. Mac-

Fenty and his wife are shocked by the trio's arrangement, all the more since their son, Horton, idolizes Rumson and wishes to adopt his lifestyle. In the meantime, news spreads that the gold supply is exhausted and it seems the town will soon be deserted. Rumson cooks up a scheme via which he and some friends can recuperate the gold dust that prospectors have been letting accumulate under the planks and floorboards of the saloon and other establishments over the years. They need only dig a network of tunnels under the entire town. Elizabeth, won over by the MacFentys, rejects her life of sin and shows both men the door. The town, literally undermined, just as literally crumbles and the predicted exodus starts soon after. Rumson decides to take his chances elsewhere, leaving Elizabeth and Pardner to find a life for themselves on their new land.

Clint Eastwood's memories of the shoot, which took place over the course of five months in Baker, a town in southern Oregon "not much bigger than a television studio," are not pleasant. Eastwood found the atmosphere so boring that he resorted to renting a farm where he raised pigs and reminisced about Don Siegel with his co-star Lee Marvin. Marvin knew

With Ray Walston, Jean Seberg,
Lee Marvin, and Harve Presnell

With Jean Seberg and Lee Marvin

68

Siegel, who had not only given him his first break, in 1952 in *Duel at Silver Creek,* but had also cast him in one of his best roles, in *The Killers* in 1966. The two men couldn't help recalling their work with this efficient director, since Joshua Logan, the man in charge of the colossal machine that was *Paint Your Wagon,* did not appear to be overly efficient. The film was going over its generous budget of $14 million, and nobody seemed satisfied with the director—to such an extent that the July 22, 1968, edition of the *Los Angeles Times* announced that Logan would soon be replaced by Richard Brooks. And yet Joshua Logan, one of the French film critics' favorite whipping boys, did not seem to be the only one to blame in this affair. By the time it was brought to the screen, Alan Jay Lerner and Frederick Loewe's musical comedy was already more than a bit outdated, and screenwriter Paddy Chayefsky had an enormous adaptation job on his hands. What's more, Paramount had been counting on Julie Andrews to make this musical a success, but she had preferred to follow Blake Edwards into the adventure of *Darling Lily.* And, finally, the nature of the production itself entailed rash expenditures such as daily plane and helicopter trips to shuttle in actors or drop off their spouses. This sort of thing disgusted Eastwood so much that he later declared, ''They spent twenty million dollars and you can't even see it on the screen.''

Be that as it may, one thing is certain—for the first

time Eastwood made a radical departure from his trademark image. The cool, laconic killer gave way to a naïve and generous young cowboy who seduced Jean Seberg with a smile and didn't hesitate to burst into song—on not one but two occasions, with ''I Talk to the Trees'' and ''I Still See Eliza.'' These two numbers were a throwback to Eastwood's early career, when he had sung on *Rawhide* and even recorded a record on the Gothic label. American critics praised his baritone and judged that Eastwood came out of the whole thing looking best. The French critics were more impressed by Lee Marvin's third-rate acting and tended to find Eastwood inexpressive and wooden.

The film's failure—along with that of *Darling Lily*—nearly sank Paramount. Only the Malpaso Company, which had loaned out Eastwood at premium rates, came out on top. Be that as it may, this attempt to recycle his image ended up as a failure for Eastwood. As for the film itself, one can give it the benefit of the doubt in view of Eastwood's remarks: ''I saw that film in three different versions—the director's version, the producer's version, and then the studio execs' version, and of all the versions, the director's, the first one, was actually the best one. But that wasn't the one that was released.''[1]

1. David Downing and Gary Herman, *Clint Eastwood, All-American Anti-Hero* (New York: Omnibus Press, 1977).

70

Two Mules for Sister Sara

1970

Distribution: Universal
Producers: Universal/Malpaso; Martin Rackin and
    Carroll Case
Director: Don Siegel
Screenplay: Albert Maltz, based on a story by Bud
    Boetticher, ''Two Guns for Sister Sara''
Director of Photography: Gabriel Figueroa (Tech-
    nicolor/Panavision)
Music: Ennio Morricone
Editing: Robert F. Shugrue and Juan José Marino
Set Decoration: Pablo Galvan

CAST:

Shirley MacLaine: *Sara;* Clint Eastwood: *Hogan;*
Manolo Fabregas: *Colonel Beltran;* Alberto Morin:
General Leclair; Armando Silvestre: *first American;*
John Kelly: *second American;* Pedro Armendariz,
Jr.: *young French officer;* Ada Carrasco; Pancho Cor-
doba; José Chavez; Pedro Galvan; José Espinosa; En-
rique Lucero

In Mexico, during the era when the Juaristas sought
to expel the occupying French, an American mercenary named Hogan kills a group of bandits as they're
about to kill a woman. The lady in question is a nun,
Sister Sara, sought by the French Army for aiding the
Juarez partisans. Hogan, intrigued by Sister Sara's
personality, agrees to escort her to safety. In the
course of the trip Hogan is surprised to see the good
sister drink abundantly and shocked to hear her swear
freely. She manages to convince him to help her dynamite a convoy carrying provisions for the French.
In the course of the attack, Hogan is wounded by an
Indian's arrow; Sara nurses him. The next phase of
the journey should enable them to join up with a
group of Juaristas preparing to attack a French-held
fortress. On the run, they take refuge in a brothel,
where Hogan discovers that ''sister'' Sara is in fact a
prostitute. That in no way affects his decision to help
the Mexicans. The attack on the fort is victorious. At
the end of the battle, Sara and Hogan declare their
love and hit the trail together.

During the filming of *Where Eagles Dare,* Eastwood
became friendly with Richard Burton and Elizabeth
Taylor, and he mentioned the possibility of doing a
film with Elizabeth. She agreed to the idea but

backed out at the last minute because she had signed another contract—and also, it seems, because she didn't find the prospect of a four-month shoot in Mexico very encouraging. Therefore, Shirley Mac-Laine replaced her in the spring of 1969 in a film where, according to Eastwood, "the woman has the best part—something I'm sure Shirley noticed. It's kind of *African Queen* gone West."[1] The comparison with *The African Queen* proved accurate on at least one point: The entire cast and crew became ill during production, except Eastwood, whose diet consisted mostly of fresh fruit.

Two Mules for Sister Sara was an old Bud Boetticher project which he had never managed to produce. Albert Maltz, one of the Hollywood Ten, wrote the screenplay for this $4 million production which left Siegel with the memory of two particularly

well-rendered passages: "Joe Cavalier, my assistant director, took a crew into the desert to get the opening credit shots with various animals in the foreground and Clint riding in the background. I told him what I wanted and it took him two weeks to get it, but it was worth it because it established a feeling for the kind of animalistic man who was our hero. . . . I also liked the battle sequence, the attack on the fort. . . . I worked very hard at making that battle sequence work because there was really nothing in the story that justified it. My goal was to make it justify itself by being very exciting."[2] *Two Mules* also left Eastwood with a lasting memory, that of the scene where Sara removes an arrow from his shoulder. "That," he says, "was the best scene I've ever played. Some critic in a small town told me once that he didn't like that scene, and I said, 'Well, you'd better give up on me, then,

With Don Siegel and with Shirley MacLaine

because that's the best I can give out.'"[3]

Two Mules marked a new twist in Eastwood's career. To all appearances, he is once again the stubble-faced mercenary of his Sergio Leone days, and the Mexican setting vaguely suggests the backgrounds of his European efforts. Even Ennio Morricone's score reinforces this impression. But, this time around, the adventurer is controlled by a woman. Sister Sara is pulling the strings and the "marionette" does her bidding. Even when he discovers that Sara is a prostitute, he rises above his ridiculed male pride and follows her on her mission, however extreme. As Siegel put it, "At the end, he's one of Sara's mules." Yet, once again, this plain evidence goes unaccepted. David Downing and Gary Herman think that the film is misogynistic since the woman is deceitful, and that Eastwood's first mistake is to believe in Sara, a nun, i.e., a nonwoman.

This sentimental comedy, featuring an intimate relationship played out against a spectacular backdrop, is a tender tale where two societal outcasts—a mercenary and a whore—find love in the midst of a revolution. (Much of the tone can no doubt be attributed to Albert Maltz.) It would have been obvious that this is a leftist film, if only Eastwood had not been blindly considered a reactionary. For Stuart Kaminsky, "*Two Mules* and *The Beguiled* are considerations of the possibility of survival for the previously unemotional Eastwood character who is willing to enter the world of pain and pleasure."[3] An impression which Siegel confirmed by stating, when the shoot was over, "Clint insists on being an anti-hero. I've never worked with an actor who was less conscious of his good image."

1. *Focus on Film*, Spring 1972.
2. Alan Lovell, *Don Siegel* (London: British Film Institute, 1975).
3. Stuart Kaminsky, *Clint Eastwood* (New York: New American Library, 1974).

Kelly's Heroes

1970

Distribution: MGM
Producers: Gabriel Katzka and Sidney Beckerman
Director: Brian G. Hutton
Screenplay: Troy Kennedy Martin (original working title: *The Warriors*)
Director of Photography: Gabriel Figueroa (Metrocolor/Panavision)
Music: Lalo Schifrin
Editing: John Jympason
Sound: Cyril Swern and Harry W. Tetrick
Length: 146 minutes
Shot in Yugoslavia and the United States

CAST:

Clint Eastwood: *Kelly;* Telly Savalas: *Big Joe;* Don Rickles: *Crap Game;* Donald Sutherland: *Oddball;* Carroll O'Connor: *General Colt;* Gavin MacLeod: *Moriarty;* Hal Buckley: *Maitland;* Stuart Margolin: *Little Jeff;* Jeff Morris: *cowboy;* Richard Davalos: *Gatowsky;* George Savalas: *Mulligan;* David Hurst: *Colonel Dankhopf;* John Heller: *German lieutenant*

During World War II, near the city of Nancy, a soldier named Kelly learns from an imprisoned German general of the existence of a tidy little pile of money—$16 million in gold—held in a bank fifty kilometers behind enemy lines. Taking advantage of his captain's three-day absence, Kelly recruits men by suggesting that they risk their lives for something a tad more interesting than the defense of French soil. His plan is to steal the gold, bury it, and return to split it up after the war. The major "volunteers" and their motivations are as follows: Sergeant Big Joe, because he can't prevent his men from following Kelly anyway; a soldier named Crap Game, because he can always manage to acquire whatever weapon is needed; and a tank driver dubbed Oddball, who's as devoted to amphetamines as he is to music. The group crosses enemy lines after having inflicted serious losses on the German army. Word of their exploits reaches General Colt, a megalomaniac who considers his men to be heroes and counts on profiting from their reflected glory. Kelly and his men end up in Clairemont, where the gold is hidden. A German panzer guards the bank and General Colt comes to the rescue from the opposite side of town. The French populace mistakes Colt for Eisenhower and the General does nothing to dissuade them in their belief, accepting their homage. During the ensuing celebration, Kelly convinces the panzer commander that it's better to have a share of the booty than to die for a lost cause.

With Don Rickles

Right after shooting was wrapped up on *Two Mules for Sister Sara,* Eastwood embarked on a five-month shoot in Yugoslavia for a film provisionally entitled *The Warriors.* The director was Brian G. Hutton, who had also directed *Where Eagles Dare.* Here was an extravaganza with comedy and satire; in one scene Hutton went so far as to make sly reference to Leone by borrowing Morricone's music.

The shooting proved difficult. Karli Baumgartner, the man in charge of special effects, used real dynamite, providing cast and crew with some memorable moments. But somewhere along the way, the film veered off the track. Eastwood told *Playboy* in 1974: "I was disappointed in *Kelly's Heroes.* That film could have been one of the best war movies ever. And it should have been; it had the best script, a good cast, a subtle antiwar message. But somehow everything got lost, the picture got bogged down in shooting in Yugoslavia and it just ended up as the story of a bunch of American screw-offs in World War Two. Some of the key scenes got cut out. I even called up Jim Aubrey, who was then the head of

MGM, and said, 'For God's sake, don't run that picture for the critics until Brian, the director, has had a chance to do some more work on it. You're going to cut off maybe millions of dollars in box-office receipts.' Aubrey said he'd think it over, but I'm sure when he hung up the phone, he said to himself, 'What does this frigging actor know about millions of dollars? Forget it.' It was released without further work, and it did badly.''

The film's message was, a priori, clear. Kelly's men became heroes for a fistful of dollars and not for defending a free Europe. It is interesting to note that, from this film on, Eastwood would defend the director's right to final cut. Director Hutton on Eastwood: "I think we went twenty years of film, from 1947, when Brando hit, until 1967, when Clint hit, with actors who, for the most part, played characters who were confused, not sure of themselves, unable to cope. Clint's character has always been a guy who knows who he is, knows what he wants and goes out and does it. Regardless if he's good or bad, he's at least certain.''

The Beguiled

1971

Distribution: Universal
Producers: Universal/Malpaso; Don Siegel
Director: Don Siegel
Screenplay: John B. Sherry and Grimes Grice (pseudonyms for Albert Maltz and Irene Kamp), based on the novel by Thomas Cullinan
Director of Photography: Bruce Surtees (Technicolor/Panavision)
Music: Lalo Schifrin
Editing: Carl Pingatore
Art Director: Alexander Cavalier
Length: 105 minutes

CAST:
Clint Eastwood: *Corporal John McBurney;* Geraldine Page: *Martha Farnsworth;* Elizabeth Hartman: *Edwina Dabney;* Jo Ann Harris: *Carol;* Mae Mercer: *Hallie;* Pamelyn Ferdin: *Amy;* Darleen Carr: *Doris;* Pattye Mattick: *Janie;* Peggy Drier: *Lizzie;* Melody Thomas: *Abigail*

The setting is somewhere in the South, during the Civil War. Amy, ten years old, is gathering mushrooms in the forest when she comes across a Union soldier, John McBurney, prostrate in agony, badly wounded with a broken leg. She manages to help him hobble as far as the home for young ladies where she

With Jo Ann Harris

77

With Pamelyn Ferdin

even sets young Amy against him by killing her pet tortoise. Now the women are frightened of McBurney. On Martha's orders, Amy goes to gather mushrooms which are prepared for dinner. McBurney is the only one who eats them. During the meal he apologizes for his behavior and expresses his desire to marry Edwina. Faced with the women's horrified expressions, McBurney realizes that he has just been poisoned. He attempts to stand and keels over, dead. The women bury him the following day. The mushrooms may not have been lethal after all, and McBurney's death was more likely due to a heart attack.

During the filming of *Two Mules for Sister Sara*, Clint Eastwood came across a novel by Thomas Cullinan, the rights to which belonged to Universal. No sooner had Don Siegel read the book and found it "exciting," than the two men decided to make the film, with the Malpaso Company handling a large share of the production. Shot in ten weeks in New Orleans, *The Beguiled* marks yet another attempt for Eastwood to shake off "The Man with No Name." A successful attempt, if one considers that *The Beguiled* is Don Siegel's masterpiece. An unsuccessful attempt, if one takes into account the film's commercial failure.

lives. The director of the home, Martha Farnsworth, agrees to help, after Edwina, her assistant, convinces her that an arrest in his present condition would mean certain death for McBurney. The boarders, excited by events, are divided as to what should be done. Doris, who harbors a vivid hatred for the North, wants to turn him in; Carol, on the other hand, dreams of seducing him. McBurney, lone man in this bevy of women deprived of men since the start of the war, takes full advantage of the situation by seducing Martha and then Edwina who, possisive by nature, is convinced that she's just met the love of her life. McBurney transforms the dreary lives of his companions; he imagines that he holds them under his spell and throws caution to the winds. Edwina catches him in bed with Carol and pushes McBurney down the stairs. The fall badly damages his now-healed leg, which Martha decides to amputate in order, so she says, to save his life. Horrified to discover the amputation when he comes to, McBurney accuses the women of mutilating him in order to keep him there among them. Furious, he announces that his word will be law on the premises and that he will choose his future mistresses at his own convenience. He

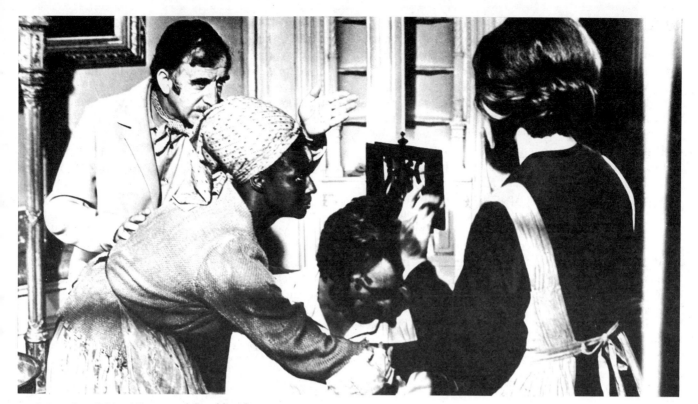

With Don Siegel, Mae Mercer, and Geraldine Page

This failure can be chalked up to two major causes. The first, highly pragmatic in nature but true in the long run, can be summed up by a remark made by producer Jennings Lang: "Maybe a lot of people just don't want to see Clint Eastwood's leg cut off." It follows that they didn't particularly want to see him die at the end, either. The second cause was a poor release strategy using misleading advertising. Eastwood wanted a modest first run, with an effort made to prepare the public for his altered image. Instead, the ad campaign was overblown and emphasized the premise that Eastwood had never before found himself in such a frightening situation—while it led people to believe that he'd get out of it alright. "It was advertised to appeal to the kind of people who were my fans from the action pictures," Eastwood told *Playboy,* and they didn't like seeing me play a character who gets his leg cut off, gets emasculated. They wanted a character who could control everything around him. The other people, those who might have liked the film, never came to see it. But it was good for me in a career sense, because it did give the few people who saw it a different look at me as a performer."[1]

For his part, Siegel considers *The Beguiled* to be "the best film I have done, and possibly the best I will ever do. One reason that I wanted to do the picture is that it is a women's picture, not a picture for women, but about them. Women are capable of deceit, larceny, murder, anything. Behind that mask of innocence lurks just as much evil as you'll find in the members of the Mafia. Any young girl, who looks perfectly harmless, is capable of murder."[2] Written by Albert Maltz (under a pseudonym, since he too disagreed with the idea of killing off Eastwood) and Irene Kamp, the film oscillates between several genres and comes across as more of a "gothic tale" than a western or psychological drama.

The opening shots are in black and white, before changing to sepia and then to color. A half-dead soldier meets a little girl who is going to save him by bringing him to a boarding school for young ladies. The realistic opening imagery, in which the war dominates, is followed by color footage of an enclosed locale where the war has not, seemingly, penetrated. It is an idyllic vision for a dying man, far from home and long deprived of his family life and sex life. But the dream soon turns to a nightmare. The soldier falls into a nest of female vipers who will castrate him before returning his mortal remains to the earth. Seen from this angle, the story could summarize the agonized perceptions of a dying man, symbolizing the final few instants before death. Siegel underlines the perfect symmetry: "We begin with black and white and end with black and white; we start with Clint and the mushrooms, and end with them; we start with Clint practically dead, and end with him dead."[2] But the film should not be taken as a "misogynistic nightmare" as it was by Judith Crist.

In fact, according to the analysis of French film critic Alain Garsault, the film is an account of the death of the male in American society. Everything which has to do with men takes place outside the confines of the boarding school; these are images (dirty ones) of war and destruction; man is basically destructive. Everything which has to do with women unfolds within a protected area, still fertile; they cultivate the soil and safeguard a peaceful space in the middle of a vast external chaos. The man's intrusion destroys the reigning harmony; a harmony which will only be restored when the males are eliminated: meaning the soldier, but also the tortoise, which the little girl from the beginning of the film has protected out of sympathy, and which will be destroyed by the soldier. The parable is clear: Males destroy themselves among themselves. Apart from his own kind, the soldier dies from *fear* that he's been poisoned—since the mushrooms were probably not lethal. Man dies from the violence he carries within himself. And as if all this were not sufficiently clear, the film is framed by a song which makes the theme explicit. Its lyrics explain that war transforms a man into a crow (and at that very moment we see a crow held captive "for its own good"), and when the crow dies (when the women lower the corpse into the ground, we see the feathered creature dead), the dove takes flight.

"This song is a definitive illumination of the film," assures Garsault. "At the time of the Vietnam war, it advises young men not to carry weapons."[3]

The Beguiled represents an important turning point in Eastwood's career. For once the critics acknowledged his acting ability. And yet, for the actor, "My role in *Beguiled* was easier to play than the lone Westerner was. In those Leone films, I had to establish an image for the audience while saying very little. In *Beguiled*, I was dealing with straight, normal emotions from my own standpoint, which were simply those of survival."[1]

Let us add that Eastwood had thought first of Jeanne Moreau, then Anne Bancroft, for the role ultimately portrayed by Geraldine Page, and that the cinematography marked the beginning of Eastwood's collaboration with Bruce Surtees, son of the great cameraman Robert Surtees.

1. *Playboy,* February 1974.
2. Alan Lovell, *Don Siegel* (London: British Film Institute, 1975).
3. *Positif,* no. 130, September 1971.

With Pamelyn Ferdin and Mae Mercer

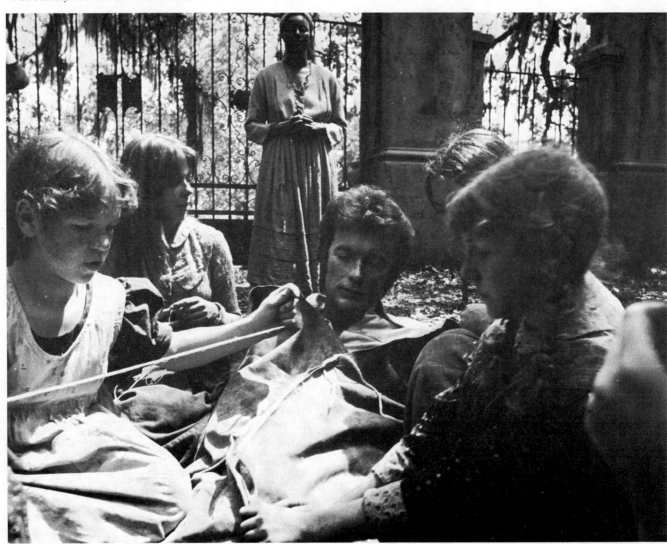

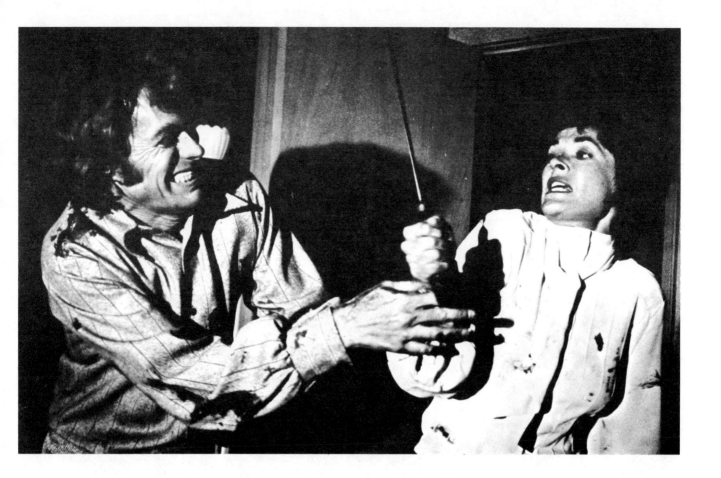

Play Misty for Me

1971

Distribution: Universal
Producer: Universal/Malpaso; Robert Daley
Director: Clint Eastwood
Assistant Director: Bob Larson
Screenplay: Jo Heims and Dean Riesner, based on a story by Jo Heims
Director of Photography: Bruce Surtees (Technicolor)
Music: Dee Barton; "Misty" composed and performed by Erroll Garner, and "The First Time Ever I Saw Your Face" sung by Roberta Flack
Editing: Carl Pingatore
Art Director: Alexander Golitzen
Sound: Woldon C. Watson, Robert Martin, and Robert L. Hoyt
Length: 102 minutes (cut down to 95 minutes)

CAST:
Clint Eastwood: *Dave Garland;* Jessica Walter: *Evelyn Draper;* Donna Mills: *Tobie Williams;* John Larch: *Sergeant McCallum;* Jack Ging: *Frank Dewan;* Irene Hervey: *Madge Brenner;* James MacEachin: *Al Monte;* Clarice Taylor: *Birdie;* Don Siegel: *Murphy, the bartender;* Duke Everts: *Jay;* Britt Lind: *Angelica;* Ginna Patterson: *Madelyn;* George Fargo; Mervin W. Frates; Jack Rosslyn; Malcolm Moran

Dave Garland is the most popular DJ in Monterey, California. The departure of his girlfriend, Tobie Williams, has left him available for romance. One of his listeners regularly phones the station and asks Garland to play the song "Misty" by Erroll Garner, for her. One night, at his friend Murphy's bar, the Sardine Factory, which is more or less his hangout, Dave meets his mysterious fan. Evelyn Draper is a liberated woman who admits to having planned their meeting. She invites him to spend the night, assuring him that it'll be just a one-night stand. But, in the days that follow, Evelyn shows up at Dave's at all hours of the day and night, without having been invited. Dave begins to find her overwhelming and disturbing, as she flies into fits of rage at the slightest annoyance.

Tobie returns to town and Dave decides to see her again. The couple renew their relationship. Evelyn is still after Dave, and he accepts an invitation to eat dinner at her house. Dave announces that he wants to call it off between them and Evelyn becomes furious. Dave returns home, and, when Evelyn phones to apologize, he hangs up without even talking to her.

Dave spends the following day with Tobie. That evening Evelyn barges into Dave's house and slits her wrists in the bathroom. A doctor friend treats the young woman and advises Dave not to leave Evelyn alone. But when Birdie, the cleaning woman, wakes him up the next morning, Evelyn is gone. She returns, however, and insults a radio producer who wishes to hire Dave. Furious, Dave sends Evelyn packing. He tells Tobie the whole story. Returning home, he finds Birdie stabbed nearly to death, Evelyn dazed and disoriented, and the presence of the police in the person of one Sergeant McCallum. Evelyn is taken off to a psychiatric hospital.

Some time later, Dave receives a new call from Evelyn. She's been cured, is about to depart for Hawaii, and asks him to play "Misty" for her, one last time. That same night Dave is awakened by the sound of "Misty" coming from his own phonograph and narrowly escapes a knife attack by Evelyn, who manages to escape. Dave notifies Sergeant McCallum and asks him to watch out for Tobie. He realizes later that the new roommate Tobie had told him about is none other than Evelyn. He dashes over to Tobie's house and stumbles into McCallum's body with a pair of scissors jammed into its chest. Tobie is tied up inside the house. In order to free her, Dave must

With Jessica Walter

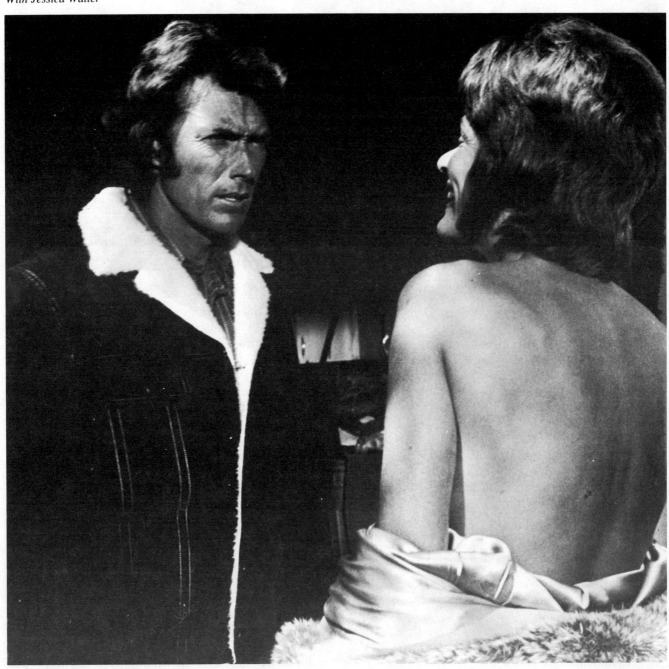

With Donna Mills

confront Evelyn one last time. She's waiting for him with a knife in her hand.

Directing was not a new idea for Clint Eastwood when he succeeded at putting together *Play Misty for Me*. His urge to direct went all the way back to his *Rawhide* days, during a specific episode: "We were shooting some vast cattle scenes—about two thousand head of cattle. We were doing some really exciting stampede stuff. I was riding along in the herd, there was dust rising up, and it was pretty wild, really. But the shots were being taken from outside the herd, looking in, and you didn't see too much. I thought, we should get right in the middle of this damn stampede. I said to the director and producer, 'I'd like to take an Arriflex, run it on my horse and

go right in the middle of this damn thing, even dismount, whatever—but get in there and really get some great shots, because there are some beautiful shots in there that we are missing.'"[1] The producer explained that the union wouldn't allow that sort of thing. Eastwood didn't give up. He asked Eric Fleming, his *Rawhide* co-star, if he'd object to Eastwood directing an episode. With Fleming's consent, the producer gave Eastwood permission to film a "coming attractions" segment for the show. But when the time came to shoot the actual episode, CBS refused, arguing that several other actors had directed episodes of their own series and that it hadn't worked to their advantage. In Sergio Leone's films Eastwood managed to obtain the right to rewrite his English dialogue. And Eastwood's ideas found their way into

Don Siegel's films as well: "The times I've directed him we would end up shooting scenes we called 'Clintus shots,' scenes which were Clint's ideas that I'd steal," recounts Siegel,[2] whose adaptations became "Siegelini" shots. At that time Eastwood even shot a short film about Don Siegel, but claims he did nothing more than turn another guy's ideas into images.

So it was that when his friend Cheryl ("Jo") Heims showed him a sixty-page treatment which would become the scenario for *Play Misty for Me,* Eastwood didn't hesitate to take an option on it. This was around the time of *Where Eagles Dare*. "I had taken it to Gordon Stulberg at CBS, and he said,

'We're doing a film here called *The Sterile Cuckoo* with Liza Minnelli. It's too much like that.' I took it to Universal—they said, 'I don't think so.' I took it to David Picker at United Artists and he turned it down. Everybody turned it down. At that time I was just starting to come into my own with my films, but I was still the kid from Europe. I didn't have quite enough juice to pull it off."[1] Cheryl Heims had a chance to sell the script and, in need of money, asked Eastwood if he would cede his option, which he did. But the film was not made.

Back at Universal two years later to make *Two Mules for Sister Sara,* Eastwood asked what had become of the project. He was told that it had been set

aside and would never be made. He then went to Jennings Lang, who responded with "Jesus Christ, who in the hell wants to see Clint Eastwood play a disc jockey?" Eastwood finally obtained Lew Wasserman's permission to make the film after explaining that he could bring it in at a very low budget by shooting in existing locales. Wasserman brought up one last objection: "Why would you want to do a film where the woman is the best part in the film?"

As soon as Eastwood agreed to forgo a salary in exchange for a straight percentage of the future profits, he got the green light. One last obstacle: Directors Guild rules required that two directors sign Eastwood's union card. Don Siegel was the first to do so. Eastwood then hired Siegel to play the role of a bartender, and began shooting with those scenes. "I wanted somebody who'd be more nervous than I was," he explained later. Nasty gossip insinuated that Eastwood lacked confidence and required Siegel on hand as a guide. But as soon as his scenes were shot, Siegel left the set affirming that Eastwood had matters firmly in hand and wouldn't have any further need for him.

Eastwood chose Jessica Walter for the grueling female lead after having seen her in Sidney Lumet's *The Group,* and against the advice of the studio, which suggested he use someone better known. Shooting took four weeks, and was conducted entirely in natural settings in Carmel, California. The film earned back several times its total budget of $750,000 and was to reach cult status on college campuses.

Play Misty for Me gives us insight into Clint Eastwood's personality from several points of view. First of all, as observed by French journalist Pascal Mérigeau: "It might seem odd that as soon as a woman makes a film, that fact alone, according to some people, means that the work merits the widest possible interest. Whereas nobody has taken much notice of the fact that 'Macho Mr. Eastwood' fought long and hard to produce a film which happens to have been written by a woman. Better still, the destructive enthusiasm of our sisters in the movement hasn't cooled one bit. Be that as it may, in the meantime, it seems that the film casts a bit of light on Eastwood's views on the relationship between the sexes, and that this conception is far removed from the image we've worked so hard to give him."[3]

And what is this concept of the relationship between the sexes? Quite simply, equality. The woman played by Jessica Walter sets up the game and makes the rules. If she's doomed in the end, it's because she's unable to handle her freedom. "*Misty* was a suspense sort of psychodrama, with an added element," Eastwood explains. "It looked at that whole problem of commitment, that misinterpretation of commitment between a man and a woman. The girl who wrote it based it on a real-life story, on a girl she

once knew. It appealed to me, too, because I've had this situation happen to me in my own life, this thing of having somebody clinging and clutching at you, not allowing you to breathe."[4] Is Eastwood an individualist? Without a doubt. But he recognizes the right of any person, man or woman, to lead his or her life as he or she sees fit. Which doesn't exactly add up to the definition of "macho." In fact, in his films and remarks, Eastwood has never stopped proclaiming the superiority of women. (This was to become even more obvious in *Breezy*.) The man gets trapped in stereotyped situations; it's the woman that humanizes him and opens him up to life.

The second point of interest is that for his directorial debut Eastwood chose a popular genre, the thriller, making use of the principles of entertainment and suspense. He stepped into a tradition (that of *Psycho*), at the same time setting himself apart by exercising different options, as in his refusal to give a psychoanalytic explanation for his main character's neurosis, or in his visual explicitness in the scenes involving violence.

Point number three: Eastwood made use of video technology during shooting. A video attachment on the Panavision camera recorded each scene, which the director could then immediately view in video playback, affording him the opportunity to make adjustments in framing or camera movement. At that time only Jerry Lewis was employing a similar technique, using a television camera mounted parallel with the movie camera. Directing is not a hobby for Eastwood; he is an actor-director who stays on the cutting edge, trying out new hardware as soon as it hits the market.

If this first trip behind the camera attracted the interest of several hesitant critics, it didn't make a dent in the hard knot of those "unconditionally opposed" to Eastwood. Two examples: Pauline Kael summed it up as "a romantic thriller for an emotionless killer." And in France, Dominique Maillet wrote: "Clint Eastwood has added his mediocrity to a ludicrous script."[5]

1. *Focus on Film,* no. 25, Summer-Fall 1976.
2. *Focus on Film,* no. 9, Spring 1972.
3. *La Revue du Cinéma,* no. 335, January 1979.
4. *Playboy,* February 1974.
5. *La Saison Cinématographique,* 1972.

Dirty Harry

1971

Distribution: Warner Bros.–Seven Arts
Producer: Warner/Malpaso; Don Siegel
Executive Producer: Robert Daley
Director: Don Siegel
Assistant Director: Robert Rubin
Screenplay: Harry Julian Fink, Rita M. Fink, Dean Riesner, based on a story by H. J. and R. M. Fink
Director of Photography: Bruce Surtees (Technicolor/Panavision)
Music: Lalo Schifrin
Editing: Carl Pingatore
Set Decorator: Robert de Vestel

Art Director: Dale Hennessy
Sound: William Randall
Length: 103 minutes

CAST:

Clint Eastwood: *Inspector Harry Callahan;* Harry Guardino: *Lieutenant Bressler;* Reni Santoni: *Chico;* Andy Robinson: *Scorpio, the killer;* John Larch: *Chief;* John Mitchum: *DeGeorgio;* Mae Mercer: *Mrs. Russel;* Lyn Edgington: *Norma;* Ruth Kobart: *bus driver;* Woodrow Parfey: *Mr. Baunerman;* James Nolan: *liquor store proprietor;* Maurice A. Argent: *Sid Kleinman;* Jo De Winter: *Mrs. Willis;* Craig G. Kelly: *Sergeant Reineke;* John Vernon: *the mayor*

The setting is San Francisco. An unidentified man perched on a rooftop fires at a woman swimming in a pool below, and kills her. That same day the police receive a ransom note from "Scorpio," demanding $100,000. If he doesn't receive the stated amount, he'll commit a murder a day, starting with a priest, or perhaps a black. Lieutenant Bressler and the mayor inform Inspector Harry Callahan that the ransom demand has been accepted. Harry displays his dissenting opinion. He is assigned a young assistant named Chico, in order to curb his bellicose tendencies. Harry and Chico tail a man whom they believe to be the killer. He gives them the slip, leaving Harry to fend off a band of hooligans.

Meanwhile, the police discover the body of a young black, shot to death with a rifle. Harry thinks the killer will return to the scene of the crime, as a challenge. Harry lies in wait to ambush him, but the criminal manages to get away. The police receive a new message from Scorpio. He has buried a young girl alive, her oxygen supply is limited, and only $200,000 delivered by Harry himself, in person and solo, will save her. All the same, Chico follows Harry and keeps in contact with him via walkie-talkie. The killer leads Harry on an elaborate itinerary. Finally Scorpio, disguised by a ski mask, attacks Harry, overpowers him, and is on the verge of killing him when Chico intervenes. The killer wounds Chico; Harry manages to sink his knife into Scorpio's thigh, handle deep, before passing out.

Harry finds the hospital where Scorpio had himself treated and learns that he lives in the Kezar Stadium guardhouse. Under the full illumination of the deserted playing field by night, Harry corners Scorpio and beats and tortures him until he reveals where the kidnapped girl is. But the police are too late—she's already dead. The district attorney harshly criticizes Harry's illegal methods and, for lack of evidence, releases the killer. In a drug deal gone wrong, Scorpio is beaten to within an inch of his life, whereupon he informs the press that it's Harry's doing. Police brutality is publicly repudiated. Harry predicts that the killer will strike again.

After having beaten up and robbed a shopkeeper, Scorpio hijacks a schoolbus full of kids and demands a ransom and a plane, ready to take off, in exchange for the hostages. On the road to the airport, Harry leaps off a bridge onto the roof of the bus. Scorpio fires through the roof, as the bus swerves out of control. When the bus comes to a halt, Scorpio makes a run for it, taking a young boy hostage. But Harry gets his man with his .44 Magnum. Disgusted, he throws aside his badge.

According to Stuart Kaminsky, *Dirty Harry* was originally conceived at Universal, where Jennings Lang had proposed it to Paul Newman, who replied that he didn't feel himself capable of playing that sort of character. Sold to Warner, the film was envisioned as a vehicle for Frank Sinatra, with Irvin Keshner as director. But Sinatra had to undergo hand surgery and was unable to participate. The subject was then suggested to the Malpaso Company. Eastwood accepted and brought in Don Siegel. The two men hired Dean Riesner to modify the script to their specifications.

Shot entirely on location in San Francisco (only the bank robbery was shot in a studio), half the time at night, *Dirty Harry* provided Eastwood with his most popular role (by January 1974, the film had brought in $16 million in box-office receipts) as well as his most action-packed. The actor performed his own stunts on the pretext that resorting to a stunt double would be cheating and would detract from the character's credibility. Opposite Eastwood, newcomer Andy Robinson (none other than the son of Edward G. Robinson) explodes onto the screen in the role of the sadistic killer. Early in 1974, Eastwood told *Playboy:* "Harry is my favorite role to date. That's the type of thing I like to think I can do as well as, or maybe better than, the next guy."

And just what is "the type of thing" that Eastwood pulls off better than the next guy? Playing a hard-nosed, cynical cop (Dirty Harry) who revolts against laws he sees as too soft for a hardened criminal and who doesn't hesitate to make use of the most expedient methods for eliminating him. "Harry's very good at his job and his individualism pays off to some degree. What I liked about playing that character was that he becomes obsessed; he's got to take this killer off the street. I think that appealed to the public. They say, 'Yeah, this guy has to be put out of circulation, even if some police chief says, 'Lay off.' The general public isn't worried about the rights of the killer; they're just saying get him off the street, don't let him kidnap my child, don't let him kill my daughter."[1]

Made at a time when peace demonstrations and anticop films were in full bloom, *Dirty Harry* was well received by the majority of policemen. Siegel and Eastwood were even invited to speak at police conferences. Surprised by the political impact the film generated, both men turned down such offers. But the social phenomenon was there. *The New Yorker* described the film as fascist. At the same time it figured on *Time* magazine's "ten-best" list, and the ultraliberal *Rolling Stone* passionately defended it.

In France, reactions were roughly the same. Alain Garsault, who had so vehemently stood up for *The Beguiled,* pounced on the film's "reactionary style."[2] From *Dirty Harry* on, the image of Eastwood as being dangerously reactionary—that is, fascist—crystallized. For Tristan Renaud (*Les Lettres Françaises*) "Calling for a police force of this kind boggles the mind"; for Gérard Lenne (*Télé 7 Jours*) it's a film stamped through with "dubiousness and dishonesty"; for François Maurin (*L'Humanité*)

"The extreme right-wing ideology is functioning at full force." And finally, for G. Lauris in *Politique Hebdo,* "Clint Eastwood, straightforward with his steely blue gaze, is a noble successor to American heroes like Wayne and Heston, violent and disenchanted, a scrapper, surely an ex-Marine."

The film stirred up such controversy that the two "perpetrators" would sound off for some time to come. "There's a reason for the rights of the accused," says Eastwood, "and I think it's very important and one of the things that make our system great. But there are also the rights of the victim. . . . The symbol of justice is the scale, and yet the scale is never balanced; it falls to the left and then it swings too far back to the right. That's the whole basis of *Magnum Force.*"[1] Siegel was taken with the notion of efficiency: "I took the situation as it existed without going into the raison d'etre for the killer's action. I wasn't interested in his background. All I was interested in was that he was a killer. Why he became a killer was left behind, because it represented dead footage for me, at least in a picture of this type."[3]

For Siegel, the "bad guys" are always more interesting than the "good," which accounts for why he renders them so brilliantly. As for Harry, according to Siegel, he's "a bigot, a bitter man. He doesn't like people. He has no use for anyone who breaks the law, and he doesn't like the way the law is administered. This doesn't mean I agree with him."[3]

Eastwood had this to say about accusations of fascism: "I don't think *Dirty Harry* was a fascist picture at all. It's just the story of one frustrated police officer in a frustrating situation on one particular case . . . this was a film that showed the frustrations of the job, but at the same time, it wasn't a glorification of police work."[1] And furthermore: "Those who say that it's a fascist film are just reveling in big words. . . . We Americans prosecuted war criminals at the Nuremberg trials because people had followed the law without taking moral consequences into account. And we judged them on this basis: they shouldn't have followed the law and their political leaders. They should have listened to their consciences. And it's on that basis that we sent them to prison. It's the same thing with Harry. When people tell him 'Things are done this way' and he replies 'Well, you're wrong, I can't go along with that' that's not a fascist attitude, it's exactly the opposite."[4]

In fact, *Dirty Harry* was constructed like a Western, which is why there is no female lead ("a love story would have slowed down the suspense," says Eastwood). It is also, as Alan Lovell points out, a film which regroups three literary themes. There is the "hard-boiled" tradition with Harry up against a world of violence and moral corruption, the "gothic" touch of the killer, straight out of some horror story, and the "social journalism" aspect which attests to an urban violence of frightening proportions. It is this last influence which leads the film

90

into its ideological aspect. The "hero" is on the side of law and order, and the assassin represents the urban element which cannot be controlled (the killer has long hair, has no permanent residence, wears a peace-sign belt buckle—all the telltale signs of hippiedom). That aside, it's a film that sets out to be a fast-moving piece of entertainment, and Eastwood asked Dean Riesner to modify the script to play up Eastwood's screen persona. At that time, the role he still felt he played best was "The Man with No Name," taciturn and quick on the draw, as imagined by Sergio Leone. Harry is an avatar of that fellow: He is alone, without a past (we barely pick up in passing that his wife is dead), and he does battle with everyone and everything. At the end, after having killed Scorpio, he tosses away his badge. The camera zooms back, leaving him isolated. As Stuart Kaminsky points out, there is no future for Harry. And if Harry did return to the screen, it was out of Eastwood's desire to respond to his critics in *Magnum Force*.

It would be pointless to deny that *Dirty Harry* is an ambiguous film. But it would be equally pointless to deny that the character is a far from positive one. Like Coogan, Harry has lost his prisoner, feels responsible in face of the law, and makes mistakes. But, as opposed to Coogan, Harry is not humanized through experience. In their final confrontation, Harry and Scorpio share their mania for destruction—they are both above the law. Coogan returns home to the country after learning a lesson from his adventures in the big city. Harry throws away his badge; he's gone too far to "return" to society.

"In radical 1972," wrote Paul Nelson in *Rolling Stone*, "the idea of a cop-as-genre-hero seems subversive to many, and, as a result, both Siegel's primary intentions and the nature of Eastwood's character have been widely misunderstood and badly distorted. . . . By the movie's end, Harry Callahan seems an archetype of the action hero adrift at the end of the 1960s, a man first and a political symbol not at all, as dignified, as honorable, and yet as out of place in today's world as are William Holden, Ernest Borgnine, Warren Oates, and Ben Johnson in theirs at the close of Sam Peckinpah's *The Wild Bunch*."[5]

Just for the record, Siegel became ill and Eastwood directed two scenes: the confrontation with the homosexual in the park and the ledge-edge rescue of the would-be suicide.

1. *Playboy,* February 1974.
2. *Positif.*
3. Alan Lovell, *Don Siegel* (London: British Film Institute, 1975).
4. "The Man With No Name" (television broadcast), BBC, February 23, 1977.
5. *Rolling Stone,* March 2, 1972.

Joe Kidd

1972

Distribution: Universal
Producer: Universal/Malpaso; Sidney Beckerman
Executive Producer: Robert Daley
Director: John Sturges
Screenplay: Elmore Leonard, based on his original concept "Sinola"
Director of Photography: Bruce Surtees (Technicolor/Panavision)
Music: Lalo Schifrin
Editing: Ferris Webster
Length: 110 minutes

CAST:

Clint Eastwood: *Joe Kidd;* Robert Duvall: *Frank Harlan;* John Saxon: *Luis Chama;* Don Stroud: *Lamarr;* Stella Garcia: *Helen Sanchez;* James Wainwright: *Muigo;* Paul Koslo: *Roy;* Gregory Walcott: *Sheriff Mitchell;* Dick Van Patten: *hotel owner;* Lynne Marta: *Elma;* John Carter: *Pepe Hern;* Joaquin Martinez; Ron Sable

The setting is New Mexico at the turn of the century. A group of Mexican peasants, long victimized by the exactions of rich American landowners—one Frank Harlan, in particular—choose a leader, Luis Chama, to plead their case before the judge of the tiny village of Sinola. But the judge is on the take. Seeing this, the Mexicans rebel and the judge's life is saved by Joe Kidd, who happens to be in court to be sentenced for drunkenness. Harlan hires a group of professional killers to decimate Chama's band, and calls upon the services of Joe Kidd as a trail guide. At first Kidd turns down the offer, refusing to participate in a manhunt. But later, when he discovers that Chama has stolen his cattle, Kidd accepts the job. Kidd is soon disgusted by Harlan's attitude and methods and so joins the Mexicans, helping them to do in Harlan and his hired guns. Equally disapproving of Chama's acts, however, Kidd manages to convince him to turn himself in to be judged by due process.

Joe Kidd, produced by Clint Eastwood, is a return to the Western. Ever fond of the genre, Eastwood probably couldn't resist the urge to be directed by John Sturges, the man who had made such classics as *Escape From Fort Bravo, Backlash, Gunfight at the O.K. Corral, The Law and Jake Wade, Last Train from Gun Hill, and The Magnificent Seven.* What's more, the film was scripted by Elmore Leonard, who, with *Hombre* and *Valdez* to his credit, ranked as one of the best contemporary writers on the West.

Nothing could have been more traditional than this story of a gunfighter who takes up the cause of the oppressed Mexican peasants in their struggle against a big landowner. Unfortunately, at the time *Joe Kidd* was made, John Sturges was on the decline and visibly looking for a second wind by returning to his preferred genre. In order to win over the public, he made concessions to the easy-going modern approach and settled for a repeat rendition of the character that had made Eastwood famous, without looking to add depth. *"Joe Kidd,"* wrote André Moreau, much to the point, in the French entertainment weekly *Télérama,* "is a fashionable blend of spaghetti westerns, which frequently resort to gratuitous violence, and the modern American western with its fascination for sophisticated firearms." Which is as good a way as any to say that this is a transition film for Eastwood, which proves that he's capable of holding his own in the company of actors such as Robert Duvall, Don Stroud, and John Saxon. We should point out that at the time, when the genre was completely moribund, Americans considered *Joe Kidd* to be a Democratic western in the face of Republican westerns such as *Chisum* and *Cahill—U.S. Marshal,* directed by Andrew V. McLaglen and starring John Wayne.

With Stella Garcia

High Plains Drifter

1973

Distribution: Universal
Producers: Universal/ Malpaso; Robert Daley
Executive Producer: Jennings Lang
Director: Clint Eastwood
Assistant Director: Jim Fargo
Screenplay: Ernest Tidyman
Director of Photography: Bruce Surtees
(Technicolor/ Panavision.)
Music: Dee Barton
Editing: Ferris Webster
Art Director: Henry Bumstead
Sound: James R. Alexander
Length: 105 minutes

CAST:

Clint Eastwood: *The Stranger;* Verna Bloom: *Sarah Belding;* Marianna Hill: *Callie Travers;* Mitchell Ryan: *Dave Drake;* Jack Ging: *Morgan Allen;* Stefan Gierasch: *Major Jason Hobart;* Ted Hartley: *Lewis Belding;* Billy Curtis: *Mordecai;* Geoffrey Lewis: *Stacey Bridges;* Scott Walker: *Bill Borders;* Walter Barnes: *Sheriff Sam Shaw;* Paul Brinegar: *Lutie Naylor;* Richard Bull: *Asa Goodwin;* Robert Donner: *priest;* John Hillerman: *bootmaker;* Anthony James: *Cole Carlvi;* William O'Connell: *the barber;* John Quade: *Jake Ross;* Jane Aull: *townswoman;* Dan Vadis: *Dan Carlin*

With Chief Dan George

The story takes place around 1870. A mysterious stranger shows up in Lago, a small town in the American Southwest. Something about the stranger is unsettling to the locals. At the saloon he is provoked by three men whom he proceeds to cut down in cold blood. Asleep in his hotel room the man is haunted by a strange nightmare: A sheriff, flat on the ground, is savagely whipped to death by three men who conduct their fatal beating before a group of cowardly citizens who, deaf to the victim's cries, do nothing to help.

The city council, including the owners of the gold mining concerns in the region, face a serious problem: Three killers, recently freed from prison, are headed for the town where they intend to torch property and spill blood in revenge against the company which had them put away. Desperate, the town calls upon the stranger, who accepts, provided he's given carte blanche to do things his own way. He proceeds to promote an oft-ridiculed dwarf to the post of sheriff, then, before the outlaws arrive, he has the town repainted bright red. Lago is now called "Hell."

When the three men hit town, the stranger is nowhere to be seen, and they proceed to carry out their vengeance. But suddenly the tail of a whip encircles the neck of one, the second is found hanged, the third is shot down as he attempts to flee. The stranger has accomplished his mission. Before blending back into the misty desert from whence he came, the stranger stops at the cemetery where the headstone on the sheriff's grave has remained without an inscription. The stonecarver, awestruck and uneasy, suddenly seems to recognize the apparition before him.

For his second directorial effort, Eastwood had an entire small town built to order on the banks of Lake Momo in northern California. Since the set was to burn at the end, the story was shot in chronological order and editing took place at the same time. The project wrapped up in six weeks. Once again Eastwood made use of a video camera on the set to monitor his work. *High Plains Drifter* was written by Ernest Tidyman, the creator of the black detective Shaft and recent recipient of an Oscar for *The French Connection.*

Drifter is a baroque western and a great many misunderstandings crystallized around it. In response to the producers, who accused him of not being sufficiently "present" in *Play Misty for Me,* Eastwood awarded himself a solid lead which required his almost constant presence on the screen. As a result, this time around he was accused of being too much in

evidence—a reproach which is partly justified. *High Plains Drifter* is an incontestably narcissistic film, right on the edge of megalomania.

But this approach is understandable when one takes into account that the film is an allegorical fantasy: The ghost of a murdered man returns from the realm of the dead to avenge himself on the cowardly town which let the murderers do their dirty deed. The cinema of fantasy makes allowances for excesses which would be unacceptable in a realistic context. Just to complicate matters further, the version of the film released in France, aiming, no doubt, to make the first level of meaning easier to grasp, gave the character an altogether different identity. So it is that the stranger has come to town to avenge "his brother," whereas in the original English-language version the stonecarver gazes upon the stranger exactly as if he's seeing a ghost. The meaning is explicit. The slow rhythm, wide-screen cinematography, and thundering music all refer back to the films of Sergio Leone. (These references were to be held up as acts of plagiarism.) As in the Leone films, the hero here has no name, as indicated by this exchange of opening dialogue:

"What did you say your name was?"

"I didn't say."

Yes, the character in *High Plains Drifter* is none other than the man from *A Fistful of Dollars*. And Eastwood will explain from whence he came and who he really is. He came from nothing and no-

With Billy Curtis

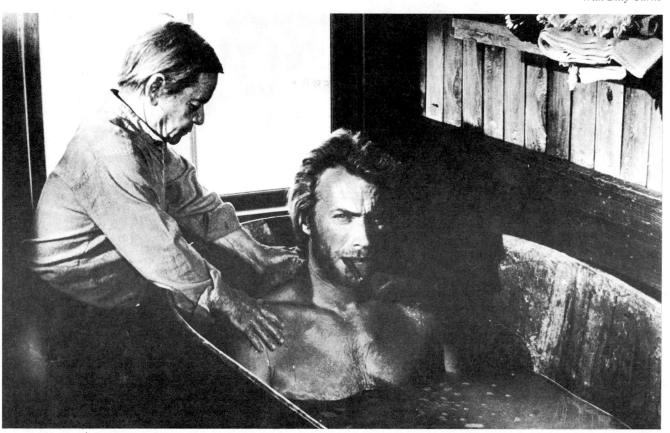

95

where, he has no name, no social context, no background, and he's a ghost.

High Plains Drifter is a final farewell to the spaghetti western (Eastwood's next Western, *The Outlaw Josey Wales,* would have a specific historical context), and a confession of the character's "unreality." The cynical hero is nothing more than a flamboyant specter on whose tomb the actor has come to perch one last time. Those who disliked the film—often fans of gory movies with bloody special effects—criticized *Drifter*'s violence without stopping to realize that it was intended as pure fantasy. To drive the point home, two of the tombstones in the cemetery bear the names *S. Leone* and *Donald Siegel*. Eastwood had himself photographed with Verna Bloom in this wry setting and used the shot to launch the *Drifter* publicity campaign. This was obviously his way of saying, with humor, that he had assimilated the influence brought to bear by the two directors who had created his image and could now stand on his own two feet. (The first film of the new independent Eastwood would be *Breezy*.)

Drifter carries with it another, more questionable aspect—that of the townspeople's cowardice. Still, Eastwood goes a bit far in comparing his film to *High Noon*. The French critical establishment lashed out at *High Plains Drifter*. "An apology for fascism," said Jean-Claude Guiguet in *La Revue du Cinéma*. "The

perfect Nazi hero," wrote Guy Tesseire in *L'Aurore*. "Typical Nazi ideology . . . the handsome blond Aryan, Clint Eastwood," wrote J. Sorel in *Témoignage Chrétien*. "A *Mein Kampf* for the West," according to Albert Bolduc of *Positif*, who went on to add: "Back in 1950, not *one* scene, not a single *shot* of this film would have obtained Universal's stamp of approval." It should be pointed out, in passing, that this last remark was courageously published under a collective pseudonym.

To all of which Jacques Zimmer was prompted to retort: "It is peculiar to see the term 'extreme right-wing,' i.e., Nazi, ideology applied to the good old-fashioned theme of a lone man come to settle an unjust score in a place where he's been named marshal out of shear fear. I won't go to the trouble of filling countless pages with the list of Westerns that revolve around these two themes. The same scenario, produced by Kramer as *Invitation to a Gunfighter,* was unanimously hailed as a parable against racism and violence."[1]

Debatable as its narcissism, haughtiness, and masochism may be, *High Plains Drifter* remains, above all, a provocative film, seductive by virtue of its baroque quality and (as in the town repainted red and renamed "Hell") its folly.

---

1. *La Revue du Cinéma*, no. 335, January 1979.

Breezy

1973

Distribution: Universal
Producers: Universal/ Malpaso; Robert Daley
Executive Producer: Jennings Lang
Director: Clint Eastwood
Assistant Director: Jim Fargo
Screenplay: Jo Heims
Director of Photography: Frank Stanley
(Technicolor)
Music: Michel Legrand
Editing: Ferris Webster
Sound: James R. Alexander
Length: 107 minutes

CAST:

William Holden: *Frank Harmon;* Kay Lenz: *Breezy;*
Roger C. Carmel: *Bob Henderson;* Marj Dusay:
Betty; Joan Hotchkis: *Paula;* Jamie Smith Jackson:
Marcy; Norman Bartold: *Man in car;* Lynn Borden:
Frank's friend; Shelley Morrison: *Nancy;* Dennis
Olivieri: *Bruno;* Eugenie Peterson: *Charlie;* Lew
Brown: *police officer;* Richard Bull: *doctor;* Collins
III: *Norman;* Don Diamond: *maître d'hôtel;* Scott
Holden: *Veterinarian;* Sandy Kenyon: *agent;* Jack
Kosslyn: *driver;* Mary Munday: *waitress;* Frances
Stevenson: *saleswoman;* Buck Young: *Paula's friend;*
Priscilla Morrill: *client in clothing store;* Earle: *Mr.
Love-a-lot*

Frank Harmon, fiftyish, directs a real estate agency
in Los Angeles and lives in a splendid house just outside town. His divorce from a shrewish woman has
left him without illusions and he lives alone, leaning
toward misanthropy. One day he picks up a seventeen-
year-old hitchhiker, Miss Breezeman, nicknamed
"Breezy." She has no fixed address, no profession,
and leads a vagabond life much like that of the hippies
she hangs out with. She is a bit wary of Harmon, since
she's already had an unpleasant experience with a
driver who tried to molest her. And although Harmon's not immune to her charms, he's not quite sure
what to say to her. Their tentative sympathetic vibes
are short-lived, however, for Breezy runs off when
she sees Frank's total indifference to a dog lying
wounded on the side of the road. A short time later,
Frank turns back, picks up the dog, and takes it to a
vet.

Later that night, Frank is mildly annoyed to find
Breezy at his door. She claims to have left her guitar
in his car, convinces Frank to let her in, and then
wheedles her way into taking a bath. But when she
asks to stay the night, Frank refuses and sends her on
her way. The following evening, two policemen
bring Breezy over and ask Harmon to confirm that
he's her uncle. Realizing that she'll be arrested for
vagrancy if he tells the truth, Frank gives in and
agrees to put her up for the night.

Despite himself he feels more and more attracted
toward her. But Frank is afraid of this idyll. He feels
uncomfortable when he runs into friends with Breezy
in tow, and can't come to terms with his relationship
to her. His old friend Bob Henderson, a bachelor em-
bittered by his own failures at romance, makes fun of
Frank. A chance encounter with his ex-wife only
serves to point out how ridiculous his relationship
with Breezy is, and Frank decides to call the whole
thing off.

Not long there after, a very dear friend tells him of
her husband's death in a car accident. Fully realizing
this woman's fear of being lonely, coupled with what
he's seen of Henderson's lifestyle, Frank sees how
vain principles are in the face of love. He heads off
in search of Breezy and finds her in a park. He suggests that she live with him for a year and that they
take things as they come without pinning their hopes
on the future.

Shot entirely on location in and around Los Angeles
for the comparatively low sum of $750,000, *Breezy*
confirmed Eastwood's desire to be a director and,
paradoxically, simultaneously confirmed the refusal

With William Holden

of the studios, the critics, and the public to accept him as such. To this day, *Breezy* remains the only film which Eastwood has directed without also playing a starring role. *Play Misty for Me* and *High Plains Drifter* had been successes for Universal because Eastwood had not only directed but starred in them. Eastwood behind the camera was not seen as as much of a drawing card as Eastwood in front of the camera, however, and as a result the studio did very little to promote the film, which was distributed in an untimely and slipshod manner. The problem was compounded by an R rating, deemed necessary since nude breasts were in evidence (twenty states have statutes which state that showing a woman's naked breast to children is obscene). Eastwood found himself deprived of the teenage audience he had counted on, and his customary fans didn't go out of their way to see the film either. As an indirect consequence, the film came out in Paris in only one theater, in English with French subtitles, on March 26, 1975. Cinema International Corporation, Universal's overseas distributor, hadn't even seen fit to print up a poster announcing its release. It proved to be one of the least attended films of the year.

At the time, Eastwood did not cast himself in *Breezy* because he felt he was too young to play the lead and, most of all, because it was a love story, a realm into which he had yet to venture. On the other hand, he also wanted to make a film where he could devote himself entirely to the business of directing. Therefore he offered the role to William Holden, who later said that he had forgotten "what it's like to make pictures this agreeable" and that he was ready and willing to work with Eastwood again any time he asked. Eastwood chose Kay Lenz, a young television actress, for the part of Breezy. Shooting took place at record speed (they were finished three days ahead of schedule) and Eastwood took the occasion to describe his working methods to *Action*, the magazine of the Directors Guild. According to him, if the entire crew feels involved with the film they'll work twice as fast and twice as hard. "If you explain what effect you're striving for, instead of saying merely, 'Put that case over there' or 'Set up that lamp down there' your crew will become totally involved."

Written by Jo Heims, who also penned *Play Misty*

for Me, Breezy, for Eastwood, is "the story of the rejuvenation of a cynic."[1] It also figures among the most liberal films about contemporary society. Rather than sing the praises of the businessman (Holden), symbol of capitalist society, or take the side of the counterforce, (the "hippie" alternative), the film tries to understand *both* characters—their lifestyles, their whole reason for being. It lauds, one more time, the creed of individualism.

For critic Pascal Mérigeau: "To her friends, Breezy is taking up the bourgeois life, letting herself get sucked into the system. As for Frank's friends and associates, they can't imagine anything beyond a brief affair, an interlude which appears to be both threatening and enviable. The scope of sexual conformity is neatly outlined. The occasional fling is perfectly acceptable but must always be tinged with hypocrisy and held in perspective, must always respect the norm and so preserve the status quo. When Frank and Breezy decide to live together for a full year, they also decide to distance themselves from their usual circles. On the one hand they are not 'made for each other,' 'everything stands between them,' and, on the other hand, the limits they themselves set will serve to set them apart from the traditional scheme of things in which couples supposedly bond 'for life.' In this way, contrary to most films based on a similar premise, the happy ending is far from being synonymous with conformity."[2]

In conclusion, as is often the case with Eastwood, this film offers a response to critics who had a thing or two to say about another one of his films. As in *Play Misty for Me*, it is the woman who gets the game rolling and directs it toward its moments of discovery and revelation. But whereas in *Misty* the woman pursues the man in order to destroy him, here she follows a similar course with the opposite goal in mind. Breezy pursues Frank so as to save him, to awaken him not only to love but to life itself (she sensitizes him to suffering via the incident with the injured dog). In short, she literally brings Frank back to the land of the living from the dead end to which his social conformity had led him.

---

1. *Focus on Film*, no. 25, Summer-Fall 1976.
2. *Revue du Cinéma*, no. 335, January 1979.

Kay Lenz and William Holden

Magnum Force

1973

Distribution: Warner
Producers: Universal/ Malpaso; Robert Daley
Director: Ted Post
Assistant Director: Wes MacAfee *Screenplay:* John Milius and Michael Cimino, based on a story by John Milius after characters created by Harry Julian Fink and Rita Fink.
Director of Photography: Frank Stanley (Technicolor/ Panavision)
Music: Lalo Schifrin
Editing: Ferris Webster
Art Director: Jack Collis
Length: 124 minutes

CAST:

Clint Eastwood: *Harry Callahan;* Hall Holbrook: *Lieutenant Briggs;* Mitch Ryan: *Charlie McCoy;* Felton Perry: *Early Smith;* David Soul: *Davis;* Robert Urich: *Grimes;* Tim Matheson: *Sweet;* Kip Niven: *Astrachan;* Christine White: *Carol McCoy;* Adele Yoshioka: *Sunny;* Richard Devon

The setting is San Francisco. Rica, a famous mafioso on trial, has just been acquitted due to insufficient evidence. On his way home with his lawyer, Rica is killed by a motorcycle cop. Inspector Harry Callahan, who has been transferred away from the homicide brigade due to his brutal methods, makes a detour to the scene of the crime accompanied by his partner, Early Smith. He is shooed away by Lieutenant Briggs, an officer who brags about never having had to use his gun to enforce the law.

Callahan and Smith decide to go get some sandwiches for lunch at the airport cafeteria, which is run by a retired cop. Harry makes the most of his lunch break by making short work of two terrorists who happen to be holding ninety passengers hostage on a plane. While practicing on the police firing range Harry meets up with Charlie McCoy, an old colleague who's on the verge of a nervous breakdown because his wife has left him. "A hood can kill a cop—but let a cop kill a hood!" Charlie complains. Harry advises him to retire. At the shooting range Harry makes the acquaintance of four young cops—Davis, Sweet, Astrachan, and Grimes—all expert marksmen. They all tell Harry how much they admire his efficiency and courage.

The following day another mafioso is killed in his own home by a motorcycle cop who tosses a bomb into the swimming pool and kills those who happen to be there in a spray of submachine-gun fire. Hearing the news, Harry suspects that his friend McCoy

may have lost his mind and taken the law into his own hands. The executions continue: A pimp who has forced one of his "protégées" to swallow drain cleaner is cut down along the side of the road, and a drug kingpin is murdered at home during an orgy. But, while leaving the scene of the crime, the killer runs into McCoy whom he also kills. We learn that the killer is none other than Davis.

In the wake of these crimes, Harry is reinstated on the criminal brigade, under Briggs. Briggs suspects a mafioso named Palancio is behind the murders and assigns Harry to bring him in. The day of the operation, the gangsters are tipped off by an anonymous phone call. The arrest turns into a freewheeling massacre in which Sweet is killed. Harry now suspects that there is a secret organization operating within the police force. The day of the marksmanship competition, Harry borrows Davis's gun and deliberately misses one of the targets. The following night he recovers the bullet from the firing range and, comparing the bullet to those used in the slayings, now holds the proof that Davis is one of the assassins. He warns Briggs, who refuses to believe him.

Heading home, Harry finds himself face to face with Davis, Astrachan, and Grimes, who are waiting for him in the parking lot. They admit to being the "executioners" and ask Harry to join them. He refuses. He now knows that he will be one of their upcoming targets. Shortly thereafter, he escapes a bomb placed in his mailbox. His partner, Smith, is not so lucky. Forewarned, Briggs hastily steps in and brings Harry to police headquarters. En route, Briggs disarms Harry and confesses to being the chief of the "vigilantes." A final battle will pit Harry Callahan against Briggs and his death riders.

Produced by Robert Daley and directed by Ted Post, *Magnum Force* is Eastwood's way of putting matters in focus. In effect, *Magnum Force*, written by John Milius and Michael Cimino, responds to all the criticism stirred up by *Dirty Harry*.

Eastwood, in the meantime, is not one to hold back. The precredits sequence of *Magnum Force*, which makes use of one of the most famous tirades from *Dirty Harry* ("This is a .44 Magnum, the most powerful handgun in the world. It could blow your head clean off. Do you feeling lucky?") openly places Ted Post's film as a sequel to the work by Don Siegel. This is not a pleading defense on behalf of Harry, but an explanation of his comportment which sheds light on the unexplored gray areas of the character.

In Siegel's film Harry was a loner, above and beyond sentiment; he nearly let himself be seduced by a colleague's wife, but circumstances saved him from making that mistake. In *Magnum Force* Harry gives the impression that he still belongs to the land of the living; he not only ends up in bed with a neighboring Indochinese girl, but in so doing gives every indication that he's capable of sustaining a humane sexual relationship with a woman. He even lets on that he values the notion of friendship, and the ultra-professional aspect of his young colleagues tends to put him off. At the end of *Dirty Harry,* Harry tosses away his badge; he no longer believes in the profession. In *Magnum Force* he accepts his role, watches out for the city's welfare, and, should he still happen to step beyond his rights (as in the scene with the airplane terrorists), he stays within the limits of the law.

That's what *Magnum Force* is all about—the will to respect the rules of democracy. The scene on the plane is as much a provocation as it is a wish not to cop out on the preceding film. But it challenges the role of the "enforcer" who takes matters into his

own hands. The problem of the inadequacy of the law remains posed all the same through the character of McCoy, the cop at the edge of his nerves. ("These days," McCoy explains, "a cop kills a hoodlum he might as well just dump the body someplace—because those snot-nosed young bastards down at the DA's office will crucify 'im one way or another. A hood can kill a cop—but let a cop kill a hood!") This doesn't prevent Harry from reaffirming his faith in democracy when faced with the three young cops who, as fascist extremists, take their inspiration from Brazilian-style "death squads."

It strikes me as important to illustrate my point by quoting lines of dialogue from the film which are extremely clear. Harry addresses the three cops in question:

"You heroes have killed a dozen people this week. What are you gonna do next week?"

"Kill a dozen more."

"Is that what you guys are all about? Being heroes?"

"All our heroes are dead. We're the first generation that's learned to fight. We're simply ridding society of killers that would be caught and sentenced anyway if our courts worked properly. We began with the criminals that the people know so that our actions would be understood. It's not just a question of whether or not to use violence; there simply is no other way, inspector. You of all people should understand that. Either you're for us or you're against us."

To which Harry offers the telling and essential reply: "I'm afraid you've misjudged me."

As if this weren't sufficiently clear, the screenwriters include another explanatory scene, this time between the police lieutenant, who also heads the "death squad," and Harry:

"A hundred years ago in this city people did the same thing. History justified the vigilantes—we're no different. Anyone who threatens the security of the people will be executed. Evil for evil, Harry. Retribution."

"That's just fine. But how does murder fit in? You know when police start becoming their own executioners, where's it gonna end, huh, Briggs? Pretty soon you start executing people for jaywalking. Then executing people for traffic violations. Then you end up executing your neighbor because his dog pisses on your lawn."

For Harry, the solution to society's ills lies in "upholding the law." When Briggs accuses him of stagnating, of sticking to "the system," Harry retorts: "Briggs, I hate the goddamn system. But until someone comes along with some changes that make sense, I'll stick with it."

Fundamentally, Harry has not changed. He acts independently, doesn't follow orders, and takes certain liberties with the law. But this same law dictates his conduct toward and against everything. "You're

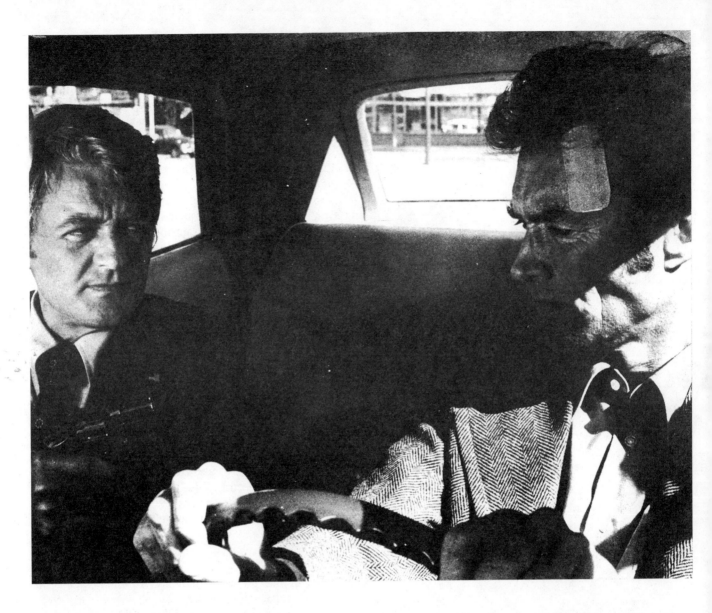

about to become extinct,'' the chief of the fascists tells Harry. To be ''extinct,'' from another era, is doubtless the very problem that Eastwood, painfully, found himself faced with. It is in this sense that he clings to the past, and it is because he respects certain values that he's labeled ''reactionary.'' In *Magnum Force* he doesn't pretend to have the answer. But he does remain loyal to the American democratic system despite its flaws and shortcomings. He finds the term ''fascist'' difficult to swallow.

Paradoxically, this doesn't change a thing as far as Eastwood's detractors are concerned. French critic Alain Garsault wrote (in the January 1975 issue of *Positif):* ''This aspect of Harry's struggle neither excuses nor modifies the film's meaning. Harry punishes the criminals he runs into the same way the four motorcycle cops punish hardened criminals. Their leader is also Harry's superior. 'Officially' a liberal man, he shows himself to be deeply intolerant. Finally, the film concludes like the others, without

really condemning the method the motorcyclists have chosen.'' Apparently we didn't see the same movie, Mr. Garsault and I.

Harry punishes the ''criminals he runs into'' by putting his life on the line in order to defend the victims. The ''hardened criminals'' are executed in a cowardly fashion without benefit of trial. As for thinking that fascism can lurk behind an ''officially liberal'' attitude, that strikes me as a fairly lucid contention while at the same time being a call for democratic vigilance. And finally, the motorcycle vigilantes *are* condemned, convicted without appeal, and even shot down by Harry because their ''choice'' has led them to accept the slaughter of innocent people, something which Harry can never accept.

A fairly mediocre directorial effort by Ted Post, *Magnum Force* is of no interest other than as an answer to the accusations made against *Dirty Harry*. Unfortunately, even when he's knocking off fascists, Eastwood is still considered dangerous.

Thunderbolt and Lightfoot

1974

Distribution: United Artists
Producers: United Artists/ Malpaso; Robert Daley
Director: Michael Cimino
Screenplay: Michael Cimino.
Director of Photography: Frank Stanley (DeLuxe/Panavision)
Music: Dee Barton
Editing: Ferris Webster
Art Director: Tambi Larsen
Length: 115 minutes

CAST:

Clint Eastwood:*Thunderbolt;* Jeff Bridges: *Lightfoot;* George Kennedy: *Red Leary;* Geoffrey Lewis: *Goody;* Catherine Bach: *Melody;* Gary Busey: *Curly;* Jack Dodson: *Bank director;* Gene Elman: *tourist;* Burton Gilliam: *Welder;* Roy Jenson: *Dunlop;* Gene Elman: Claudia Lennear: *secretary;* Bill McKinney: *crazy driver;* Vic Tayback: *Mario;* Lila Teigh; Bud Taylor: *gas station client*

Jack Thunderbolt, his true identity concealed in the guise of a pastor, is in the middle of conducting a sermon when he is run right out of his own church by two old accomplices with whom he'd committed a holdup. With the two men firing in hot pursuit, Thunderbolt is saved in the nick of time by Lightfoot, a thrill-seeking young adventurer who has just stolen a car. The two men get along right off the bat. Thunderbolt explains that he's hidden the loot from the holdup behind the blackboard of a classroom in an old schoolhouse. The new associates head there, but upon reaching their destination find that the school has been replaced by ultramodern buildings. Their two pursuers—Red, a violent, angry man, and Goody, a rather dim-witted individual—catch up with them. Thunderbolt manages to convince them of his good faith and Lightfoot persuades them all to pull off a new job together.

The four accomplices attack a bank vault with the help of a Howitzer cannon. The operation, meticulously thought out, unfolds without a hitch. But a last-minute incident puts the police on to them. Goody is killed in the chase; Thunderbolt and Lightfoot escape by posing as a couple of lovers in a drive-in (Lightfoot is disguised as a woman). They run into

With Jeff Bridges

With Jeff Bridges and George Kennedy

With Jeff Bridges and George Kennedy

Red, who, overcome with rage, knocks out Thunderbolt and savagely beats up Lightfoot, whom he leaves decked and badly wounded before beating a hasty retreat. Sighted by the police, Red tries to outrun them, but loses control of his car and goes careening through a store window. The guard dog rips out his throat.

Having managed to get away, Thunderbolt and Lightfoot accidentally discover that the old school had simply been moved in order to serve as a museum. The loot is still in place right where he left it, and Thunderbolt gets it back. He celebrates the occasion by buying Lightfoot the white Cadillac he's always dreamed of. On the road to freedom, Lightfoot succumbs to his wounds, and Thunderbolt realizes he has just lost the only friend he ever had.

During the making of *Magnum Force* Eastwood seems to have been receptive to suggestions and dialogue changes from script co-author Michael Cimino. In fact they saw eye to eye to the extent that Eastwood didn't hesitate to hire Cimino to both write and direct his next film, *Thunderbolt and Lightfoot*. The choice was a surprising one, and the decision more courageous than it seems. After all, at that time Eastwood could have been cautious and eliminated all risks by producing only made-to-measure films written by experienced scenarists who could concoct surefire scenes for him, instead of taking chances on new talent just imagine Alain Delon or Jean-Paul Belmondo handing a young director his first film on a platter). Yet, not only did Eastwood place his trust in a complete beginner ("A no-talent Michael Cimino about whom you are unlikely to hear more," wrote Rex Reed in his review for the *New York Daily News*), but he also agreed to play opposite rising star Jeff Bridges, for whom Cimino set aside the best scenes. The stupid French title of the film (*Le Carnardeur,* or *The Sniper*) as well as the poster (Eastwood hunched behind a cannon) played up, yet again, the actor's image as being virile and invincible. Never has an ad campaign been more misleading. In reality, *Thunderbolt and Lightfoot* is a totally disenchanted American ballad in the manner of *Butch Cassidy and the Sundance Kid* or *Scarecrow*. (Certain American critics even claimed to see it as a right-wing *Easy Rider*.)

Like so many Eastwood characters, Thunderbolt is a man without a past. The viewer is surprised to find him hidden in the cloak of a pastor, who is obliged to hastily take leave of his flock, while in the process of preaching the good Word, in order to avoid being slaughtered by two gangsters (George Kennedy, Geoffrey Lewis) as idiotic as they are brutal. Thunderbolt is rescued by Lightfoot, a man twenty years his junior, who has just stolen a car by pretending to be a lame Vietnam veteran, thereby playing on the uneasy conscience of well-to-do middle America in the wake of the war. Our two men hit the road in search of symbolic treasure in the venerable tradition of the "road movies" of the sixties, as well as that of the Western.

Thunderbolt and Lightfoot follow an itinerary of initiation in the course of which the "young" man learns a great deal from the "old," without, of course, any conscious effort on the part of the latter to impart moral instruction of any kind. We're obliged to wait for the second half of the film, where we discover the professional ease of the man behind the cannon, before we understand the name *Thunderbolt*. For Thunderbolt is a tired man at the end of the road who allows himself to be carried along by Lightfoot. Lightfoot kids around, even gets ahold of a girl for his buddy, but Thunderbolt wants above all to be left alone in peace. Hell-raising, love-making, and outings with friends no longer seem to suit a man of his age. He's not macho, not a womanizer, not even a fighter, really.

Cimino makes use of the two men's path through the mountains of Montana and Idaho to paint several entertaining vignettes. We're shown girls smashing the cars of the guys who have tried to pick them up, while a frustrated hunter takes dozens of rabbits out of his trunk so he can try to now them down with a rifle. The film has the allure of a laid-back, farfetched comedy where the absurdity of life is confirmed around every bend in the road. But this is America, and however lush and magnificent the countryside, it does a poor job of hiding the latent fear and violence. A holdup, planned in the spirit of a hoax, suddenly takes a dramatic turn and the spectacular and inevitable car chases are punctuated by all-too-real injuries and by death itself. The two gangsters may come across like country bumpkins, but they are part of the American heartland, and the ridicule that follows their every move does nothing to prevent their intolerance and their killing. This will be made only too clear to Lightfoot, who looks at life as a joke. It is significant that he is beaten to death while disguised as a woman. In the end his getup marks him as being on the fringe and provokes his elimination at the hands of a dullwitted gangster, a "virile" warrior.

Thunderbolt and Lightfoot skillfully blends several genres: the thriller, the comedy, the action film, even the "morality play." After *Breezy,* this is Eastwood's new tribute to peace and friendship in the face of the violence the world has to offer.

With Jeff Bridges

The Eiger Sanction

1975

Distribution: Universal
Producers: Universal/ Malpaso; Robert Daley
Executive Producers: Richard D. Zanuck and David Brown
Director: Clint Eastwood
Assistant Director: Jim Fargo
Screenplay: Warren B. Murphy, Hal Dresner, and Rod Whitaker, based on the novel by Trevanian.
Director of Photography: Frank Stanley (Technicolor/Panavision)
Music: John Williams
Editing: Ferris Webster
Art Director: George Wedd
Sound: James R. Alexander and Aurelio Crugnola
Length: 128 minutes
Shot partly on location in the Swiss Alps

CAST:

Clint Eastwood: *Jonathan Hemlock;* George Kennedy: *Ben Bowman;* Vonetta McGee: *Jemima Brown;* Jack Cassidy: *Miles Mellaugh;* Heidi Bruhl: *Mrs. Montaigne;* Thayer David: *Dragon;* Reiner Schoene: *Freytag;* Michael Grimm: *Meyer;* Jean-Pierre Bernard: *Montaigne;* Brenda Venus: *George;* Gregory Walcott: *Pope*

Jonathan Hemlock, university art professor and inveterate fan of fine painting, has assembled a personal collection of remarkable and valuable canvases by carrying out a series of contracts for an undercover agency which is presided over by an unnerving albino named Dragon. Dragon sends a lackey to contact Hemlock so as to offer him an important sum to sanction (in layman's terms: kill) two enemy agents who have killed one of Dragon's agents. Hemlock, who has been lusting after a Pissarro for some time, agrees to kill one of the targets provided he receives $20,000, twice his usual fee. Jonathan accomplishes his mission in Zurich and, upon his return to the U.S., finds himself obliged to accept the second sanction. The exact identity of the target is not known, but Dragon has managed to learn that the man in question will be part of an international climbing expedition which will soon attempt the north face of the Eiger, and that he also limps from time to time as a result of frostbite.

Jonathan, himself a former mountain climber, heads for Arizona to get in shape under the tutelage of his old friend Ben Bowman, who will be running the base camp for the Swiss climbing expedition. While in training, Jonathan escapes two attacks and disposes of one of his enemies. After arriving in

Switzerland with Ben, Jonathan meets his climbing partners: Freytag, Meyer, and Montaigne. When less than a week later they begin their ascent of one of the most dangerous peaks around, Jonathan still hasn't succeeded at determining which of his associates is the killer. Ben surveys their progress through a telescope from the foot of the rock face. He's concerned not only about the disagreements Jonathan had with the group leader during preparations, but by the bad weather which is brewing. Montaigne, injured by a rock slide, dies on the morning of the third day. The group decides to call off the climb and descend with the body. Everyone except Jonathan manages to fall off the mountainside into the gaping void. The emergency rescue team, led by Ben, extricates Jonathan, who then notices that his friend is limping, but refuses to sanction him, out of friendship. Jonathan is congratulated by Dragon, who finds it quite remarkable that he made a point of killing everyone on the expedition so as to be certain of hitting the assassin.

"I took a book Universal owned—a best-seller—and I couldn't figure out what to do. The book has no ties. In other words, the character who is killed at the beginning has no relationship to anybody else. I just took it and tried to make the guy relate to the hero, so the hero had some other motivations."[1] *The Eiger Sanction,* which Universal suggested to Eastwood, is the sort of film which, due to hesitations here and there, ends up satisfying no one. Obviously the book was purchased with something James Bond-ish in mind. The writer who uses the name Trevanian is far from being a negligible author, and it's unfortunate to see incompetent studios and a fair share of the critics relegate this decent novel to the level of the most mediocre Bonds, simply because it has to do with spies.

The fundamental error doubtless starts right there. *The Eiger Sanction* was produced like a film meant to rival the grandiose espionage movies of its day. Spectacular action and visuals therefore take precedence at the expense of the psychology (a state of affairs which would provoke Trevanian into attacking Eastwood's film as "insipid" and "stupid" in his book *Shibumi*). Obviously the most spectacular thing *The Eiger Sanction* has to offer is the scenes in the mountains. After training for several days in Yosemite National Park, Eastwood made up his mind that no climbing scenes would be shot in the studio and that he would do all his own stunt work—a decision which naturally led to complications with the insurance companies. How can a top box-office star, pushing middle age to boot, be permitted to stroll around at an altitude of 10,000 feet with a sheer drop below? The impression of danger was unfortunately confirmed on the second day of shooting when David Knowles, a British stuntman, was killed by a falling boulder. Despite everything, the actor-director de-

With George Kennedy

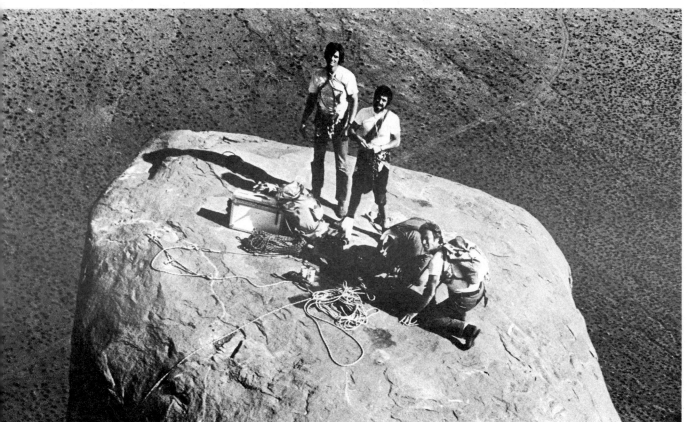

cided to continue and make the most of the film. In general he would be given credit for his athletic efforts (he is not doubled in a single climbing scene), but the weakness of the script would be just about unanimously deplored.

Certainly *The Eiger Sanction* is an uneven film, but the critical reactions it provoked leave one flabbergasted. Certain French critics especially had found their expiatory victim in Eastwood. Their hatred and contempt burst out of every sentence. All of which might seem strange if one considers that his three preceeding films were *Breezy, Magnum Force,* and *Thunderbolt and Lightfoot.* Judge for yourself:

"John Wayne has spawned millions of children. A dozen of his very own, hundreds of thousands ready to start Vietnam all over again to have his virility and, in addition, an illegitimate son, the fruit of the comically monstrous marriage between the "spaghetti western" and a fistful of dollars: Clint Eastwood. And he's one of the most dangerous offspring, since he's not stupid, as his adversaries will tell you. His clientele: the immense American Silent Majority. A slightly masochistic majority, too, it would seem, since, face it, there's no one more antipathetic than Clint Eastwood" (Michel Grisolia, *Le Nouvel Observateur,* July 25, 1975).

"Clint Eastwood, this second-rate actor who was launched to stardom in Italy thanks to Sergio Leone and the spaghetti western, has retained the mishmash of genres, a taste for pastiche and for violence at all costs, from his sojourn in the studios of Rome . . . .This spicy cocktail has its charm. It bears magnificent witness to the extent to which utter brainlessness has pervaded Western man today" (Louis Marcorelles, *Le Monde,* July 19, 1975).

"Convinced that he is pursuing the tradition of noble virility so dear to the Western and epic heroes of yesteryear, we watch Clint Eastwood create his own myth, film after film, with all the naïveté of a Boy Scout certain that his is the combat of the righteous, approved by God and by his country's Silent Major-

ity. . . . Of all the actors who have recently stepped behind the camera, Clint Eastwood is assuredly the one least encumbered by modesty" (Michel Perez, *Le Quotidien de Paris,* July 21, 1975).

". . . Which is not to say anything against Clint Eastwood the actor, who manages the nifty trick of not expressing himself half badly for a guy who won't permit himself to act" (Louis Chauvet, *Le Figaro,* August 4, 1975).

It is interesting to note that in this sampling, be one on the left or over on the right, everyone detests Eastwood. To be more precise, these reviewers oscillate between condescension and scorn. What is alarming here is not so much the savage attacks (partly merited) on *The Eiger Sanction,* but the ignorance of what Eastwood had done *before.*

This happily is not the case for Alain Garel who, writing in *La Saison Cinématographique* for 1976, underlies the dreamlike aspect of the work (i.e., the character of Dragon) and "a masterful last half hour, shot without resorting to rear projection, there, unprotected on the open slope of the Eiger." Pascal Mérigeau (*La Revue du Cinéma,* no. 335, January 1979) adds: "Eastwood's major merit here, yet again, is to not be contemptuous of the script he has agreed to make, but to do his very best to deliver quality entertainment. In so doing he gives us proof of a humility which a number of our young geniuses would do well to learn from." And finally, in regard to the meaning of the film, it strikes me as important to dwell on the "moral" of *The Eiger Sanction.* The climbing team meets its death and Eastwood is congratulated by his superior who compliments him on the ruse of knocking off the others in order to conceal the execution of the guilty party. The film ends on a shot of Eastwood, dazed that anyone would think him capable of murdering several men just to conceal his real mission.

---

1. *Focus on Film,* no. 25, Summer-Fall 1976.

The Outlaw Josey Wales

1976

Distribution: Warner-Columbia
Producers: Warner/Malpaso; Robert Daley
Director: Clint Eastwood
Assistant Director: Jim Fargo
Screenplay: Phil Kaufman and Sonia Chernus, based on the novel by Forrest Carter, *Gone to Texas*
Director of Photography: Bruce Surtees (De-Luxe/Panavision)
Music: Jerry Fielding
Editing: Ferris Webster
Production Design: Tambi Larsen
Sound: Tex Rudloff, Bert Hallberg
Set Decoration: Chuck Pierce
Stunt Coordinator: Walter Scott
Length: 135 minutes

CAST:

Clint Eastwood: *Josey Wales;* Chief Dan George: *Lone Watie;* Sondra Locke: *Laura Lee;* Bill McKinney: *Terrill;* John Vernon: *Fletcher;* Paula Trueman: *grandmother;* Sam Bottoms: *Jamie;* Geraldine Keams: *Little Moonlight;* Woodrow Parfey: *carpetbagger;* Joyce Jameson: *Rose;* Will Sampson: *Ten Bears;* William O'Connell: *Carstairs;* John Quade: *Comanche chief;* Sheb Wooley; Royal Dano; Matt Clarke; John Verros

At the outset of the Civil War, Josey Wales, a peaceable Missouri farmer, sees his wife and young son massacred by a band of Union soldiers led by a Captain Terrill, who slashes Wales across the face with his sword before riding off with his men. Left for dead, Josey Wales now lives only for revenge and joins up with a group of Confederate rebels under the leadership of a man named Fletcher. But theirs becomes a lost cause and even the last unyielding hold-outs abandon the struggle. Fletcher encourages his men to accept the amnesty offered by the North. They all give themselves up, except Josey. The whole arrangement is a trap—as soon as they've surrendered their arms, the "rebels" are massacred in cold blood. Josey only manages to rescue a badly wounded young man, still in his teens, who dies soon after.

Josey Wales, now a declared outlaw with the Yankees on his trail, heads for Indian territory and hides out on Comanche land. There he teams up with Lone Wolf, an elderly Cherokee, and together they decide to make their way to Mexico. They are soon joined by Little Moonlight (a Navaho squaw who has been unfairly banished from her tribe) and a half-starved dog. Along the way, Josey's group rescues an old woman named Sarah and her granddaughter Laura Lee from death or worse at the hands of Co-mancheros. The band of tagalongs arrive in Texas, where they set up communal housekeeping in an abandoned ranch belonging to Sarah. The property is not far from a former boom town, now nearly de-serted in the wake of the silver rush. Ten Bears, a Comanche chieftain, wants to chase out the new ar-rivals but Josey convinces him that they can all live together in peace.

Terrill and his men, who have been tracking Josey, end up surrounding the ranch. Josey and his protégés wipe out their assailants. Terrill makes a run for it—Josey catches up to him in town and kills him. Fletcher and two rangers show up, also with the mis-sion of capturing Josey. When the inhabitants of the town catch on that their new friend is in danger, they come to the rescue by addressing him as ''Wilson'' and claiming that Josey Wales is dead, or gone to Mexico. Fletcher, who has certainly recognized Josey, takes his leave saying, ''I think I'll go down to Mexico to try to find 'im. I think I'll try to tell him the war is over.''

Displeased with the poor promotion *Breezy* and *The Eiger Sanction* had received, Eastwood dropped Uni-versal in favor of Warner Bros. (who count *Dirty Harry* and *Magnum Force* among their biggest suc-cesses). *The Outlaw Josey Wales* marked Eastwood's return to the genre that had made him famous, the Western. It was both a successful return and a provi-sional farewell. *Josey Wales* is not only one of the four or five great Westerns of the seventies, it also stands as Eastwood's wish to join the true classic tra-dition of legendary heroes of the West. Having rid himself of ''The Man with No Name,'' he was ready to take his place alongside John Wayne and Gary Cooper. But, as we shall see, the pessimism of the Watergate era couldn't help but mark the film, and *Josey Wales* would prove to be more of a swan song than a renaissance for the Western.

The inspiration for the project was a first novel by Forrest Carter, a forty-six-year-old half-Cherokee In-dian poet. ''Forrest had no formal education—in-cluding grammar school. He's a terribly self-taught person who became famous as an Indian poet and teller of stories. Somebody talked him into writing one down. So he wrote this western, *The Rebel Out-law: Josey Wales* and it was published down in Arkansas by a publishing company called Whippoor-will Publishing. They put out about seventy-five cop-ies—that's all—hard cover.''[1]

Had Forrest Carter had Eastwood in mind all along? The fact remains that Carter spontaneously sent him a copy of the book without bothering to go through a literary agent or the Writers Guild. ''Some-times you don't like to take unsolicited scripts,'' says Eastwood, ''because of possible plagarism.''[1]

The book was accompanied by a letter. ''The letter was such a reaching-out kind of thing—it had such a nice feeling about it—that my associate Bob Daley figured 'Well, I've got to give this at least a twenty-page read and see if it's going anywhere.' So he sat down to read it and ended up reading through dinner and reading through the night. He called me the next morning and said, 'God, this thing has so much *soul* to it that it's really one of the nicest things I've read.' So I said, 'Get it to me right away, I'll read it.' I read it and felt the same way about it.''[1]

Eastwood proceeded to buy the screen rights. Once filming was underway the book was released in pa-perback as *Gone to Texas*, which Eastwood didn't like as a title ''because it puts it into a specific re-gion. *Rebel Outlaw* I didn't like because there are so many AIP pictures about motorcycle gangs.''[1] The film was entitled, more simply, *The Outlaw Josey Wales*. Forrest Carter has since written a sequel, *The Vengeance Trail of Josey Wales*, in which the action takes place at the end of Maximilian's rule. East-wood hired his friend Sonia Chernus and Philip Kaufman (whose film *The Great Northfield, Min-nesota Raid* he had appreciated) to adapt the work to the screen. Kaufman was also supposed to direct the film, but Eastwood took his place after a week, as a result of their profound disagreement over the nature of the character. Kaufman saw him as very down-to-earth, whereas Eastwood wanted a more ''epic'' por-trayal.

And just who is this character? Once again East-wood would model his role after a part he had al-ready played, but this time the character would be considerably enriched by a past which would enable the audience to understand his motivation. Deeply American, Eastwood had suffered from becoming fa-mous playing rootless ''heroes.'' For him, putting down roots was the only thing that could lend him human depth. *''Josey Wales,''* he explains, ''is a saga, a little like *The Good, The Bad and the Ugly*, except that in the Leone film the only character you got to know—somewhat—is the Eli Wallach charac-ter. In other words, Josey Wales is a hero, and you see how he gets to where he is—rather than just hav-ing a mysterious hero appear on the plains and be-come involved with other people's plight.''[1]

Eastwood was well aware of his ''specificity.'' Considering his screen past, it would be difficult for him to just step right into Gary Cooper's or John Wayne's boots. ''I do everything that John Wayne would never do,'' Eastwood confided to *Variety* when *Josey Wales* was released. ''I play the hero but

I can shoot a guy in the back. I react according to the circumstances at the time.'' This explains why he has a hard time accepting criticism of the violence in his films. For Eastwood, the violence is never gratuitous—it is always motivated by ''circumstances.'' According to Eastwood, Peckinpah loved violence for its own sake—if he used slow motion at the end of *The Wild Bunch* it was to accentuate its beauty. In Eastwood's work, the violence is always quick and brutal and intended to shock the viewer.

In this regard, the opening of *Josey Wales* is revealing. The violence here is extreme, bordering on provocation, as if Eastwood were saying ''You wanta see me as a bloody killer?—well, you'll get your money's worth.'' But this particular violence is historically grounded, situated as it is on the border between abolitionist Kansas and antiabolitionist Missouri during the Civil War. ''We tried to find as much information as we could about the outlaws of Kansas. We've all heard about the Missouri guerillas—a lot has been written about that, Bloody Bill Anderson and the group down there—but there hasn't been too much written about the Kansas Red-Legs. They were actually sanctioned—legal—by Missouri; they were a state militia. They were like a vigilante group who, under the guise of protection, did a lot of bad deeds.''[1]

The precredit sequence of *Josey Wales* opens on a shot of Eastwood, peaceable farmer, tilling his field. The sound of horses, off-screen, and the appearance of a column of smoke announce the brutal eruption of war and an end to all things peaceful. Josey's wife and son are slaughtered by a band of Union renegades. After having buried his family, Josey dusts off his pistols and joins up with the Confederate army. The Civil War is summarized by a montage of scenes based on vintage photos which roll under the opening credits. By the time the credits finish, the war is over. The rebels surrender and fall into a lethal trap. Josey, the last holdout, is the only one to get out alive. He beats a hasty retreat with a mortally wounded young soldier, but, when his companion dies, he finds himself completely alone with a pack of killers on his trail.

Alone against all, with vengeance in his heart, Josey Wales bears a close resemblance to the hero of *High Plains Drifter*. The story couldn't be more traditional up to this point. But if *High Plains Drifter* follows a negative itinerary, beginning and ending in death, the path Josey Wales will follow is just the opposite. It commences in death and emerges into life. Twenty minutes into the film, with the viewer on familiar ground, *Josey Wales* changes its tone and turns into a picaresque ballad with a humanitarian theme.

With Sondra Locke and Chief Dan George (preceding pages)

118

While Josey, still a member of the walking wounded, is hiding out in Indian territory, he meets Lone Watie, an elderly chief whose tribe, driven off its land by the white man, has been forced to head west. Lone Watie tells Josey that he ''had a fine woman and two sons who died on the Trail of Tears'' and found himself useless on the tribal council. By accepting the old Indian as a traveling companion, Josey contributes to Lone Watie's ''resurrection'' and, without knowing it, begins to pave his own re-

turn to the land of the living.

The two men are soon joined by a young Indian woman who has been exiled by her tribe for having failed to ward off the advances of the Arapaho warriors who held her captive. And finally a dog graces them with his company. Along the way, the group saves an old woman and her granddaughter from the aftermath of a Comanchero ambush. Finally this new ''family'' reaches a small town on the Rio Grande and settles on the farm which had belonged to the old woman's son, killed in the war. All these ''cripples,'' these outcasts, these exiles, wish for only one thing—to live in peace. But the farm is on Comanche territory and the Indians are not about to accept squatters.

So it is that Eastwood introduces the film's key scene. Josey, the loner, the adventurer, can just as well cut out and leave the farmers to fend for themselves against the Indians. ''You are the gray rider, you would not make peace with the blue coats, you may go in peace," the Commanche chief "Ten Bears" tells Josey. "I reckon not," Josey replies. "Got nowhere to go." And with this reply comes an end to the solitary adventurer, an end to the hardened loner cop, an end to the hired killer of *The Eiger Sanction.* The last of the "poor lonesome cowboys" refuses to hit the trail yet again, refuses to ride down the path of adventure to court the inescapable end—be it pathetic or cast in the grand tragic mold—of the

legendary heroes of the West. He asks only to become a part of society, to join the very same "others" for whom he once professed contempt or amused condescension.

"Then you will die," replies Ten Bears.

"I came here to die with you—or live with you. Dyin' ain't so hard for men like you 'n me—it's livin' that's hard when everything you loved's been raped or massacred. Governments don't live together like men do. With governments you don't always get a fair word or a fair fight. Well, I've come here to give you either one—or get either one from you. The bear lives here, the wolf, the antelope, the Comanche. And so will we."

"It is good that warriors such as we should meet in the struggle of life—or death. It shall be life." This verbal pact for "life," sealed in blood, is all the stronger given that the Comanche chief's face is decked out in full war paint.

From that moment on, the conclusion is inevitable. Forced to take up arms against his pursuers one last time, Josey is saved by the members of his "family," as they, too, accept him as one of their own (quite the opposite of John Wayne in *The Searchers,* who finds himself excluded anew once he's brought back the niece who had been captured by Indians; and counter also to Shane's fate in the George Stevens' film of that name: Shane is obliged to take up his wandering again because "you can't live like other people once you've killed a man"). And the only man who could identify and arrest Josey pretends not to recognize him and tells him "If I meet up with Josey, I'll try to make him understand that the war is over." "I reckon so," Josey replies. "I guess we all died a little in that damn war."

The Outlaw Josey Wales is a film of reconciliation. Reconciliation between the stranger who rode out of the spaghetti Western and the traditional American Western hero of legend; reconciliation between the misanthrope and his fellow men. Josey has not only created a family, but has allowed himself to give in to love and the wish for happiness. And it is interesting to note that hate is symbolized by the vigilantes who lay down their own law while love is represented by a community of outcasts, not unlike a hippie commune. What's more, this community is accepted by its two neighbors, the Comanches and the white inhabitants of the nearby town. "And I say that men can live together without butcherin' one another," says Josey.

Shot in the course of eight and a half weeks in Utah, Arizona, and California, *The Outlaw Josey Wales* is a lyrical epic of scope and grandeur. Directing with a sure hand, Eastwood presents scenes of violence as successfully as he does more intimate passages blending comedy and melodrama. He is extremely well backed up by the performance of Chief Dan George, discovered six years earlier in *Little Big Man,* and by the presence of Sondra Locke, who had starred in Robert Ellis Miller's film *The Heart Is a Lonely Hunter* some eight years earlier and who had hardly had a part worth playing since. (Locke had also been up for the part of *Breezy.*) The film was warmly welcomed overall, and if some reviewers continued to see it as a work in praise of violence, *Time* magazine listed it among the year's ten best. Jerry Fielding's score was nominated for an Oscar.

1. *Focus on Film,* no. 25, Summer-Fall 1976.

The Enforcer

1976

Distribution: Warner-Columbia
Producers: Warner/Malpaso; Robert Daley
Director: James Fargo
Screenplay: Stirling Silliphant, and Dean Riesner, based on a story by Gail Morgan Hickman and S. W. Schurr based on characters created by Harry Julian Fink and Rita M. Fink
Director of Photography: Charles W. Short (DeLuxe/Technicolor)
Music: Jerry Fielding
Editing: Ferris Webster and Joel Cox
Art Director: Allen E. Smith
Stunt Coordinator: Wayne Van Horn
Length: 96 minutes

CAST:

Clint Eastwood: *Harry Callahan;* Tyne Daly: *Kate Moore;* Harry Guardino: *Lieutenant Bressler;* Bradford Dillman: *Captain McKay;* John Mitchum: *DiGeorgio;* DeVeren Brookwalter: *Bobby Maxwell;* John Crawford: *the mayor*

Two truckers pick up a young woman hitchhiker and escort her home with less than chivalrous intentions. But when they reach her place, a young man named Bobby kills them for no apparent reason. In San Francisco, Inspector Harry Callahan and his partner DiGeorgio are cruising their beat. Harry has just taken care of a scam in a restaurant when a new bulletin reaches them—a liquor store holdup is in progress, one officer has already been killed, and hostages have been taken. Callahan and DiGeorgio manage to get the situation under control, but the resulting shoot-out produces $14,379 worth of damage. Harry finds himself transferred to the personnel department the next day. He's bored to tears despite the presence of Kate Moore, a young and pretty auxiliary member of the force whom he tries to dissuade from becoming a detective.

During the night, the truck whose drivers had been killed pulls up to a munitions depot. Bobby and an accomplice kill the night watchman and, with the help of others hidden in the truck, load up several bazookas. They're caught in the act by DiGeorgio and his new partner. Bobby mortally wounds DiGeorgio with a knife, one of the accomplices is killed, and the gang manages to get away by running over the other detective. Harry sees his old buddy in the hospital one last time before DiGeorgio dies.

Callahan's superior, Bressler, has received a tape recording from a terrorist group threatening to carry out a series of attacks unless they receive a million dollars. Harry is put back on the homicide brigade to handle the affair. And, despite everything, his new

partner is the lovely Kate Moore. Having identified the accomplice DiGeorgio killed, Harry follows the lead, but has a falling-out with city authorities who have arrested the leader of a black pacifist group with whom Harry had made an agreement. Relieved of his duties, Harry nevertheless continues his investigation with Kate's help.

The mayor is kidnapped and his entourage is slaughtered by the terrorists, who are now demanding $5 million dollars. After a series of ups and downs Harry discovers that the terrorists are hiding out on Alcatraz Island. He and Kate manage to rescue the mayor, but Kate sacrifices her life in the process. Harry contemplates Kate's lifeless body as a voice from a police helicopter announces to the kidnappers that their ransom demand has been accepted.

According to Boris Zmijewsky and Lee Pfeiffer[1], Clint Eastwood was in no hurry to start another film after putting so much effort into *Josey Wales*. But two young people, Harry Julian Fink and Rita M. Fink, had written a film noir script with Eastwood in mind and, unable to see him personally, left it for him at a restaurant he owns in Carmel. Reading it, Eastwood saw the makings of another Dirty Harry vehicle and asked his friends Stirling Silliphant and Dean Riesner to work on adapting it. The resulting

project was entitled *Dirty Harry III*. The part was tailor-made for Eastwood, who decided to give James Fargo, who had served as assistant director on *Josey Wales,* his big break. The film was released as *The Enforcer,* a title which had already served for a Raoul Walsh/Bretaigne Windust film starring Humphrey Bogart.

Once again we see hard-nosed Harry Callahan, the guy who seems to break the law every time he tries to enforce it. The film's opening connects it to the two preceding sagas: Harry puts some gangsters very much out of commission. Eastwood's humor, which can be a trifle grating in the Dirty Harry series, is also present and accounted for. When the gangsters demand a car for their getaway, Harry obliges—by crashing right into the store with one. Unfortunately that which follows also has an air of déjà vu about it. When Harry's boss shows him the bill and criticizes the brutality of his methods, Harry delivers his trademark reply, telling him that the justice system is more concerned with the rights of criminals than with the rights of the people it's supposed to be protecting. Bumped down to personnel, Harry is called back to the force to solve an important problem (a repeat of *Magnum Force*). A terrorist group steals a stockpile of arms and ammunition and issues an ultimatum (much as in *Dirty Harry*). Add on the fact that Harry's trusty partner is fatally wounded during the theft (a throwback to *Magnum Force*) and once again you have the incorruptible inspector on the loose in search of revenge.

What else could be done to beef up the plot? Assign Harry a complete novice as a partner (as in *Magnum Force*)—and this time, make it a woman. As good a way as any for Eastwood to demonstrate, once again, that he's not a sexist. And, in effect, he has the same sort of relationship with her as he did with his partner in *Magnum Force*. It's her lack of experience he objects to, not the fact that she happens to be a woman.

More interesting still is Harry's relationship with Mustapha, the leader of the black pacifist group. Here the Inspector's point of view becomes more clear. If he detests the terrorists it's because they claim to act in the name of a revolutionary ideal when they're really nothing more than vulgar gangsters. ''Judge people not by their words but by their deeds,'' could be Harry's motto. Although he has little or nothing in common with the pacifist, Harry respects him because he is a sincere man acting in accordance with his convictions, and men of goodwill, however different they may be, should be able to understand one another. So it is that Mustapha, who refutes violence, understands Harry better than anyone. ''You're goin' out there and put your ass on the line for a bunch of dudes who wouldn't even let you in the front door—any more than they would me,'' Mustapha tells Harry.

1

2

"I'm not doing it for them," replies Harry. Asked about his deeper motivation, Harry will only say, "You wouldn't believe me if I told you."

As David Downing and Gary Herman[2] have written: "It is a great shame that Harry never has to confront an enemy like [Mustapha], one who would raise more profound questions about his own character and purpose, rather than the infinitely easier targets of corrupt and phoney officialdom and San Francisco's psychotic fringe." This remark is entirely justified as far as *The Enforcer* is concerned. This time around Harry sees everything in black and white. "Why, it's the return of Zorro!" wrote French critic Alain Garsault. "He also champions the oppressed with an idealism that remains unspoken, is just as clear-sighted, and just as invincible."[3] And critic Alain Garel accurately concludes: "Harry certainly reveals the rotten side of American society and so fits into the liberal tradition of the 'thriller' (both filmic and literary) but, by dint of Eastwood's charisma (exploited to the hilt), he becomes the deep, unformulated desire of the American collective unconscious incarnate: the providential man who, endowed with honesty and integrity, will stop at nothing to clean out the Augean Stables that are America."[4]

Directed efficiently but without any great personal flair by James Fargo, *The Enforcer*, after *Josey Wales*, is little more than a simple showcase for East-

122

wood. It marks the first time that the actor reincarnates an old character without bringing something new and different to the role. Coming at this point in his career, the film was deceptive, even useless. On the other hand, its considerable commercial success indicated that all of Eastwood's attempts to modify his screen persona had not really been understood. In the eyes of the public he remained, above all, a violent character.

1. Mark Whitman, *The Films of Clint Eastwood* (Isle of Wight: BCW, 1973).
2. David Downing and Gary Herman, *Clint Eastwood, All-American Anti-Hero* (New York: Omnibus Press, 1977).
3. *Positif*, no. 194, June 1974.
4. *La Saison Cinématographique*, 1977.

3

4

1. With Robert Hoy and Coloria Prince
2. With Tim O'Neill
3. With Tyne Daly
4. With M. G. Kelly

The Gauntlet

1977

Distribution: Warner
Producers: Warner/Malpaso; Robert Daly
Associate Producer: Fritz Manes
Director: Clint Eastwood
Assistant Director: Richard Hashimoto
Second Assistant Directors: Lynn Morgan and Peter Bergquist, Al Silvani
Screenplay: Michael Butler and Dennis Shryack
Director of Photography: Rexford Metz (DeLuxe/Panavision)
Music: Jerry Fielding
Editing: Ferris Webster, Joel Cook
Art Director: Allen E. Smith
Script supervisor: Catalina Lawrence
Special Effects: Chuck Gaspar
Jazz Soloists: Art Pepper and John Faddis
Length: 109 minutes

CAST:

Clint Eastwood: *Ben Shockley;* Sondra Locke: *Gus Mally;* Pat Hingle: *Josephson;* William Prince: *Blakelock;* Bill McKinney: *constable;* Michael Cavanaugh: *Feyderspiel;* Carole Cook: *waitress;* Mara Corday: *prison guard;* Douglas McGrath: *Bookmaker;* Jeff Morris: *policeman;* Samantha Doane, Roy Jenson, Dan Vadis: *bikers;* Carver Barnes: *bus driver;* Robert Barnett: *doctor;* Teddy Bear: *lieutenant;* Mildred J. Brion: *old woman on bus;* Ron Chapman: *old cop;* Don Circle: *employee;* James W. Gavin, Tom Friedkin: *helicopter pilots;* Darwin Lamb: *police captain;* Roger Lowe: *ambulance driver;* Fritz Manes: *helicopter marksman;* John Quiroga: *taxi driver;* John Rainer, Al Silvani: *policemen;* Art Rimozius: *the judge*

Ben Shockley is a cop with a reputation for getting the job done. His superior, Blakelock, assigns him to escort Gus Mally, "unimportant witness in an unimportant trial," from Las Vegas to the Phoenix, Arizona, City Hall. Arriving in Las Vegas, Shockley gets his first surprise when he discovers that *Gus* is short for *Augustina* and that his prisoner is a young woman. The second surprise comes when she informs him that they're both going to get killed and that folks are already placing their bets. Discovering that there is indeed money riding on Mally's head, Ben smuggles his witness out in an ambulance and requests that a car be put at his disposal along the way to the airport. When the vehicle in question blows up after the driver turns the ignition key, Ben begins to believe Gus and follows her to her place. From there he telephones Blakelock to send reinforcements. A while after, a dozen squad cars surround the house and the police open fire. This time around Ben is certain that there's a conspiracy, that someone has laid a trap for him, and that that someone might just be Blakelock himself. Ben flees with Gus, crossing the desert on a motorcycle stolen from a gang of bikers. They manage to escape a helicopter attack only to find themselves under assault from the motorcycle toughs, who have inconveniently hopped the same train as Ben and Gus, and whom they meet in an empty cattle car. Not far from Phoenix Ben telephones Josephson, the only colleague he knows he can count on, and informs him of his plan. Josephson contacts a lawyer, Feyderspiel, unaware that he's in cahoots with Blakelock. Meanwhile, Ben and Gus have stolen a bus and turned it into a makeshift armored car. They arrive at the Phoenix city limits, where Josephson meets them. He convinces them to follow him, but is shot by a trigger-happy killer. Ben and Gus head up the main street toward City Hall. An army of police opens fire on the bus but they make it to their destination all the same. Blakelock orders his men to fire. Ben forces Feyderspiel to admit that Gus is a witness for the prosecution against Blakelock. Blakelock shoots at Ben. Gus opens fire on Blakelock.

Shot on a budget of five million dollars, *The Gauntlet* is perhaps Eastwood's most serene film, the most accomplished in its control, blending extreme violence and a distancing brand of humor. It's as if, having reduced Dirty Harry to a stock character in the James Fargo film, Clint Eastwood decided to bid Harry adieu and see him off in style.

On first glance, Ben Shockley in *The Gauntlet* could be a brother to Harry Callahan, or, better yet, Harry himself a few years down the line (although in that case one would have to ignore *The Enforcer,* made only a year earlier). Ben, like Harry, is an inspector, solitary, obstinate, and incorruptible. He's singled out for the toughest missions because he has a reputation for following through, whatever the circumstances. There is one small difference: Ben is not at all meticulous about his personal appearance, he gambles, and he seems more inclined toward alcohol than to women. But these traits could be made to fit an aging Harry. Misanthropic, like Harry, Ben is dead certain that he's in the right. One doesn't go into the cop business without being damned sure of oneself. Within the first twenty minutes Eastwood puts all of Ben's sterling "qualities" in question: Obstinate might also mean narrow-minded, solitary could mean vulnerable, and incorruptible doesn't mean a whole hell of a lot when your higher-ups have become the symbol of corruption itself.

Ben, like Harry, could burrow even more deeply into his misanthropic ways. But this time someone is going to undertake his education, and through the tri-

With Pat Hingle and Sondra Locke

als and tribulations in store on this, his most difficult mission to date, Ben will wise up and find out about "real" life. Real life is literally going to smack him in the face. He will also discover love and put a few things that he would have previously considered intolerable into their proper place.

Step one: Although he gets chewed out by his superior, Ben is proud to be different. He's tough and people respect him for it. Step two: This "toughness" might be more like stupidity, and turns out in fact to be Ben's major weakness. It takes a prostitute, a woman on the bottom rung of the social ladder, to point this out to him without softening the blow: she tells him that he was given the job simply because he was the only one stupid enough to take it. And she proves her point. In the face of this revelation the "tough guy" has only one solution: to make a run for it. Step three: Things are not as they should be. The chief of police is corrupt, the "whore" is a sensitive and cultivated individual, and the whole vast law enforcement machine is rigged to kill innocents and protect the guilty. The logical conclusion to all this is a trusty old Eastwood theme: People must be judged not by their words but by their deeds. The young woman appears to be defenseless but she's capable of delivering a swift kick to the groin when necessary, or of offering herself to a gang of motorcycle thugs to help save Ben.

Whether aggressive or humiliated, the woman emerges triumphant because she is privy to the secrets of "virility" and knows its limits. The men, on the other hand, assert themselves more through talk than through action. Critic Pascal Mérigeau points out that "Eastwood really puts matters into focus in the scene where the policeman at the wheel is literally sickened after verbally provoking Gus . . . whom he happens to know makes her living as a prostitute. The mechanism of male fantasizing denounces the essential role language plays in the affirmation of virility. The man, caught in the trap of his own words, sees his argument boomerang back against him. The good citizen, the good cop he believes himself to be, has to call on moral principles to justify his own vulgar obsessions."[1]

The scene on the train is revealing in this respect. Ben, who flaunted his badge in order to give the bikers a hard time, gets the beating he deserves for having inflated his authority. He puts himself forward as strongest, in words, but the facts painfully contradict him. In sacrificing herself for him, Gus proves to Ben that the sexes aren't all that different—only their means of defense vary. Ben has learned his lesson, and shoves one of the bikers' female cronies off the train at the moment when she tells him: "You wouldn't do that to a lady!" Social statutes are abolished; only individuals count. After this episode, Ben

126

With Sondra Locke

and Gus are allied for good. (It is of note that the chief of police aims to eliminate Gus because, in availing himself of her sexual services, he believed he would humiliate her as a woman but instead ended up revealing the flaws in his own virility.)

Step four: Ben and Gus have let drop their masks of social convention. They are no longer a cop and a prostitute but two human beings in league with one another and ready to "run the gauntlet" so as to be allowed to live in peace. This title *Gauntlet,* again according to Pascal Mérigeau, represents a method whereby British officers used to whack their comrades as a disciplinary measure. "The guilty must pass between two rows of their fellows and be whacked by each one in turn. The scene in which the bus cuts across Phoenix through a barrage of police gunfire as insane as it is organized, is a modern version of the ritual thrashing except that here the goal is to kill. Shockley, made out to be a renegade, is fired upon by his own colleagues."[1] Here once again the trial is social and consists of ripping off masks. The chief of police *declares* Shockley guilty and uses public services for his personal ends. Through *action* Shockley proves that his chief is lying. And from that point on the chief is as vulnerable as the others. The conclusion only appears to be optimistic. Society is a kingdom where *appearances* rule. Ben and Gus have made society tremble by the simple act of *being*. Will

they be forgiven?

With *The Gauntlet* Eastwood's line of reasoning and especially his sense of humor finally became apparent to the French critical community. And if critic Michel Pérez considers Ben to be "the Attila who outpolices the police" (which is going a bit overboard since Ben is only trying to save his own skin and never instigates trouble), he doesn't fail to note that "he gives the others' sense of humor a good whipping" (*Le Matin,* April 12, 1978). Olivier Eyquem (in *Positif,* no. 206, May 1978) sees "the admission of a romanticism kept too long under wraps" (and yet Eastwood had already made *Breezy*). Jacques Zimmer (in *La Saison Cinématographique* for 1978) goes so far as to evoke Buster Keaton: "We're not at a loss for analogies between Ben and Buster. Consider the cold beauty, the solitude, the unremitting determination to surmount the obstacles of an impossible journey, the ingenuity, physical balance, and terseness." In any case *The Gauntlet* is a sort of exorcism for Eastwood. The heightened violence, cranked up to fever pitch, frees him for a while from the noise and fury of his preceding characterizations. After the gauntlet has been run we are left, if only for an instant, with a character at peace with himself.

1. *La Revue du Cinéma,* no. 328, May 1978.

127

Every Which Way But Loose

1978

Distribution: Warner-Columbia
Producers: Warner/Malpaso; Robert Daley
Associate Producers: Fritz Manes and Jeremy Joe Kronsberg
Production Managers: Billy Ray Smith and Ernest Wehmeyer
Director: James Fargo
Assistant Director: Larry Powell
Second Assistant Directors: Wendy Shear, Al Silvani and Alain J. Silver
Screenplay: Jeremy Joe Kronsberg
Director of Photography: Rexford Metz (DeLuxe/Panavision)
Art Director: Elayne Ceder
Musical Supervision: Snuff Garrett
Music Conducted by: Steve Dorff
Music Editor: Donald Harris
Music Mixing: Grover Helsley
Film Editors: Ferris Webster and Joel Cox
Sound Editors: Gene Eliot and Marvin I. Kosberg
Sound Effects Editor: Joe Von Stroheim
Set Decoration: Robert de Vestel
Costumes: Glen Wright
Length: 114 minutes

CAST:

Clint Eastwood: *Philo Beddoe;* Sondra Locke: *Lynn Halsey-Taylor;* Geoffrey Lewis: *Orville;* Ruth Gordon: *Ma;* Beverly D'Angelo: *Echo;* Walter Barnes: *Tank Murdock;* George Chandler: *DMW employee;* Roy Jensen: *Woody;* James McEachin: *Herb;* Bill McKinney: *Dallas;* William O'Connell: *Elmo;* John Quada: *Cholla;* Dan Vadis: *Frank;* Gregory Walcott: *Putman;* Hank Worden: *campground employee;* Jerry Brutsche: *street sweeper driver;* Cary Michael Cheifer: *manager;* Jeannette Louise Cole: *Palamino girl;* Sam Gilman: *fat guy's buddy;* Chuck Hicks: *truck driver;* Timothy P. Hirvin: *MC;* Tim Irwin: *musician;* Billy Jackson: *Better;* Joyce Jameson: *Sybil;* Al Silvani: *Tank Murdock's manager*

In California trucker Philo Beddoe's circle of friends we find Orville, who deals in wrecked cars, an orangutan won in a bet, and "Ma," a coarse and spunky old lady. Philo makes ends meet by fist-fighting local toughs. The matches are organized by Orville and betting is brisk. In a bar one night, Philo becomes enamored of country-western singer Lynn Halsey-Taylor. She seems to be captivated by Philo's personality, then disappears without a word. Philo sets out after her with Orville and Clyde in tow.

From town to town and from bar to bar Philo takes

on the local champs and makes enemies out of two cops. A decrepit gang of would-be Hell's Angels and their sour-tempered leader have made up their minds to get Philo. In the course of tracking him, the bikers lose their cycles one by one, and the two policemen end up pathetically bogged down while Orville gets sweet on Echo, a rather eccentric ex-fruit peddler. Philo finds Lynn and they spend a marvelous night together before Lynn runs off again. When Philo finds her she confesses her preference for another man. As Philo gets ready to leave town, Tank Murdock, an aging local hero, challenges him to a fight. Philo gets the upper hand, but, realizing how shattering a defeat would be for Tank, allows himself to be beaten.

Eastwood undertook the relatively costly *Every Which Way But Loose* (with a budget of five million dollars) despite discouragement from Robert Daley and the money men at Warner. Eastwood told *Variety* in January of 1979 that it had been an uphill struggle to break with the "macho" image critics had saddled him with. Eastwood's preceding films had been action-oriented with some comedy in the background. This was a comedy with a backdrop of adventures. Apparently Robert Daley worried most about the choice of supporting lead—an eleven-year-old orangutan. "I was strongly advised against shooting with an animal," explains Eastwood, "because it could prove dangerous." The trainer could not be at the ape's side nonstop, and, sure enough, one scene nearly took a turn for the worse when the ape flung itself at Eastwood while the actor was behind the wheel driving a truck. But all in all Eastwood and "the big baby" got along just fine. Eastwood told reporters that as soon as the orangutan saw that "I was the one signing the checks" it was on its best behavior.

Eastwood's advisers had good reason to be concerned about *Every Which Way But Loose:* Rarely had an actor gone so far in poking fun at his very own myth. The movie parodies Leone's films, makes fun of the police and the Hell's Angels, lets our hero fall for a vulgar golddigger, and shows him in clandestine boxing schemes—not to mention his outlandish entourage, which includes a brother with a stake in the action and a mother who leans more toward insults and brawls than the more traditional tenets of motherly love.

Nevertheless, as French critic Alain Garsault points out, "This putting in question leads neither to the destruction nor the tearing down of what Eastwood has always stood for. Eastwood still comes out a hero: Philo triumphs over all his adversaries, be they serious or pathetic, by virtue of his strength and integrity. The failed romance is forgotten as quickly as were his conquests in the other films. The moral of *Every Which Way But Loose* is more pragmatic than noble and marks a complete departure from the line his character has always taken. Philo prefers the carefree security of anonymity to a fragile and everthreatened glory."[1]

There's no question that the film encroaches on Burt Reynolds's *Smokey and the Bandit* territory. One might think that this movie was simply cashing in on a fad for "burlesque comedies based on male stars and their virile exploits. This film too is acompanied by country music with its blend of nostalgia and laughter."[1] And yet the work to follow (most notably *Honkytonk Man*) would prove that Eastwood's soft spot for an America peopled with dinky saloons and homegrown country music was sincere. The eleven songs which pop up through the film are more than background music; they complement the action and move the story along.

Be that as it may, the film is not entirely satisfying, due to a touch too much demagoguery and James Fargo's flat, rough direction. Polishing off cops and fascistic hoodlums back to back, with a flourish of ridicule, might seem like an entertaining idea, but it does little to diminish the fact that these same cops and hoodlums strike fear into the heart of America. Having Mr. Muscle Man just happen along to give these guys a good thrashing is a bit too facile. Moreover, the excessive use of close-ups, the snazzy framing, and ineffectual editing all help to accentuate the underlying vulgarity of the script and prevent the story from attaining the level of a fable.

This unpretentious entertainment, according to Eastwood, was scarcely advertised at all and was released in a large number of small towns. Contrary to all predictions, the film was a smash hit and remains Warner's fourth-biggest grosser to date behind *Superman, Superman II,* and *The Exorcist.* Eastwood's share of the profits turned out to be more than Marlon Brando's astronomical fee for *Superman.*

The film was shot down by American critics. *Variety* reached the conclusion that if Eastwood held onto his audience in the wake of this film, they would be on his side forever. This prognosis would be proven false, but at the time Eastwood looked like a sharp businessman gifted with a rare flair for pulling off a major switch at the most opportune moment.

---

1. *Postif,* no. 219, June 1979.

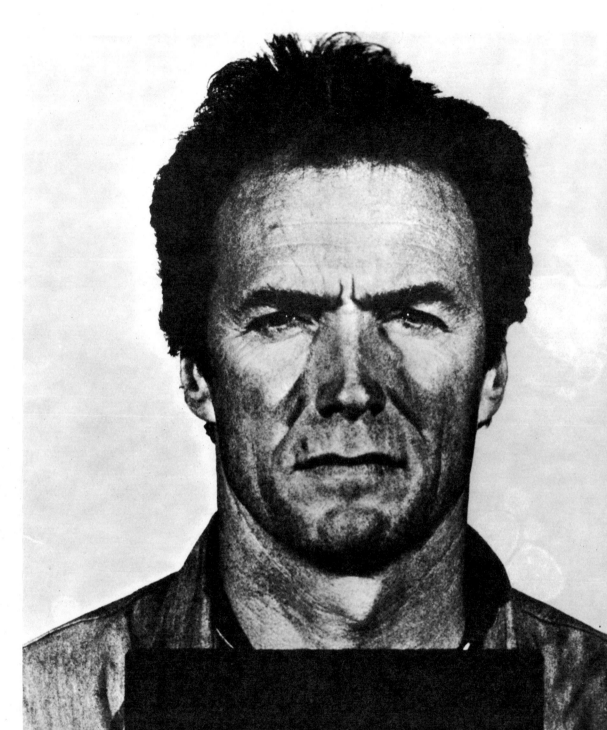

AZ 1441

FA-5033-12

Escape from Alcatraz

1979

Distribution: Paramount
Producer: Paramount/Malpaso; Don Siegel
Executive Producer: Robert Daley
Associate Producer: Fritz Manes
Production Manager: Jack Terry
Director: Don Siegel
Assistant Director: Luigi Alfano
Second Assistant Directors: M. Johnson and Richard Graves
Screenplay: Richard Tuggle, based on the book by J. Campbell Bruce
Director of Photography: Bruce Surtees (De-Luxe/Panavision)
Music: Jerry Fielding
Editing: Ferris Webster
Set Decorator: Edward J. McDonald
Assistant to Don Siegel/Dialogue Coach: Carol Rydall
Construction Coordinator: Gene Lauritzen
Sound Effects Editor: Alan Robert Murray
Continuity: Lloyd Nelson
Sound Engineer: Bert Hallberg
Music Editor: June Edgerton
Gaffer: Charles Saldana

Head Electrician: Chuck Holmes
Special Effects: Chuck Gaspar
Makeup: Joe McKinney
Costume Coordinator: Glenn Wright
Property Master: Larry Bird
Casting San Francisco: The Brebner Agency
Title Credits/Opticals: Pacific Title
Length: 112 minutes

CAST:
Clint Eastwood: *Frank Morris;* Patrick MacGoohan: *Prison Warden;* Robert Blossom: *Doc;* Jack Thibeau: *Clarence Anglin;* Fred Ward: *John Anglin;* Paul Benjamin: *English;* Larry Hankin: *Charley Butts;* Bruce M. Fisher: *Wolf;* Frank Ronzio: *Litmus;* Fred Stuthman: *Johnson;* David Cryer: *Wagner;* Madison Arnold: *Zimmerman;* Blair Burrows: *Guard (fight);* Bob Balhat-Chet: *Medical Assistant;* Matthews J. Locricchio: *Guard (visit);* Don Michaelian: *Beck;* Ray K. Goman: *Area Coordinator;* Jason Ronard: *Bobs;* Ed Vasgersian: *Cranston;* Ron Vernan: *Stone;* Stephen Bradley: *Guard (visit);* Garry Goodrow: *Weston;* Dan Leegant; John Garabedian: *guards;* Donald Siegel: *Doctor;* Denis Berkfeldt; Jim Haynie; Tony Dario; Fritz Manes; Dana Derfus; Don Cummins; Gordon Handforth; John Scanlon; Don Watters; Lloyd Nelson; George Orrison; Gary F. Warren; Joe Whipp; Terry Wills; Robert Irvine; Joseph Knowland; James Collier; R. J. Ganzert; Rob-

ert Hischfeld; Dale Alvarez; Sheldon Feldner; Danny Glover: *Guards;* Carl Lumbly; Patrick Valentino; Glenn Wright; Gilbert Thomas; Eugene W. Jackson: *Prisoners*

After having succeeded at escaping from several penitentiaries, Frank Morris is transferred to Alcatraz on June 18, 1960. Intelligent, cold, and taciturn, he has made up his mind to take his chances and escape from this model stronghold where every prisoner is under individual surveillance. Within the first few days Morris becomes friendly with Litmus, a resourceful old burglar. He also makes friends with English, a black from Alabama under life sentence for having killed two white men (who tried to kill him first), and Charley Butts, his neighboring inmate.

Frank learns the ropes at Alcatraz. After being tossed in solitary confinement for fighting off the advances of Wolf, a sadistic killer, and after seeing his pal Doc slash off his fingers with a hatchet when the warden revokes his painting privileges, Frank decides to escape. He contacts the Anglin brothers, whom he'd known in another prison, and gets things underway with Charley's help.

Working by night with nail clippers and a spoon, he enlarges the air vent in his cell, concealing it first with a suitcase and later with a casting. After a few weeks he explores the duct which leads to the platform above, which in turn is separated from the roof by a grill. Using a makeshift handcrafted drill, he breaks through one of the bars. Meanwhile the Anglin brothers and Butts have managed to dig through

their cell wall and, using rubber raincoats stolen from the cloakroom, have built a sort of life raft. The warden decides to transfer Frank to another part of the prison. Frank moves up the escape date. When the time arrives, Butts backs out, frightened. The Anglin brothers and Frank vanish without a trace. Did they perish in the escape? Even today, no one can say.

The evening of January 4, 1960, a prisoner named Frank Lee Morris was brought to Alcatraz. Morris, aged thirty-four, had been arrested on September 29, 1958, for holding up a bank in Memphis, Louisiana. This was by no means his first criminal charge. His recidivism combined with numerous escape attempts prompted his transfer to Alcatraz, the sole prison from which no one had ever escaped. Records describe Morris as nonviolent and well above average in intelligence. During the night of June 11, 1962, Morris managed to get away in the company of two other inmates. The authorities maintain that the three men must have drowned and that their bodies were carried away by the current. Not a word has been heard about them what became of them.

One year later, Alcatraz closed up for good. Journalist J. Campbell Bruce made a thorough investigation and brought out a book-length version of the story in 1963. Don Siegel, who had already made the remarkable *Riot in Cell Block 11,* discovered Bruce's book in 1966: "The theme fascinated me and I worked up a treatment called *'The Rock.'* No studio was interested at the time and I forgot the project. In 1978 I received Richard Tuggle's script which, to my great surprise (he was a beginner) pleased me enormously. Having bought it, I sent it to Clint Eastwood right away since he struck me as perfect for the part: all the characters he's played have been fierce individualists and rebels. I was particularly interested in turning Dirty Harry into a prisoner, to put him on the other side of the bars."[1] Eastwood accepted immediately: "I react to a script more by gut instinct than intellectually. In *Escape from Alcatraz* I was above all drawn to the conflict between Frank Morris and the warden and to Morris' obsession. This man had only one goal: to escape, and his exceptional intelligence had the authorities real worried, especially the warden." The prospect of working with Don Siegel again wasn't displeasing either. "Working with Don gave me a considerable feeling of freedom," remarked Eastwood at the end of shooting.[1]

There were enormous problems in store for the filmmakers—obtaining permission to use Alcatraz Island, then visited by 800,000 tourists a year, and restoring the facilities to appear as they had circa 1960

when they were still in use. The operation would cost $500,000.

Production designer Al Smith indicated Siegel's chosen point of view when he described the extent to which the location was refurbished: "The plumbing was entirely destroyed, the electrical wiring had been eaten away by humidity. We had to redo every cell—seal up broken windows, completely repaint the walls. Everything had to be brought in by boat—paint, cables, drinking water. A regular invasion. . . . For the fitting out we contacted the warden at San Quentin, a prison built around the same time as Alcatraz. With his help we were able to get our hands on almost two hundred matresses, sheets, blankets, toothbrushes, everything prison issue. It was especially important to respect the authenticity of the decor."

Although J. Campbell Bruce had retraced Frank Morris's life in some detail, Siegel was interested exclusively in his stay at Alcatraz. The title of his initial project, *The Rock,* makes this sufficiently clear. The chosen point of view is almost documentary. Only the conditions of day-to-day survival within the prison and relationships with the warden, the guards, and the other inmates are taken into account. As viewers we know nothing about the past of this prisoner brought in one stormy night except that he has a number of escape attempts under his belt—and that's all that's needed to create an atmosphere of suspense.

We get to know Morris according to Siegel's plan, analyzed as follows by French critic François Forestier: "A prisoner is brought to the warden's office. Said warden calmly trims his nails and keeps his visitor waiting. Finally he puts the nail clipper down in an ashtray which already contains another nail clipper. Then, using a scale model of the penitentiary as a visual aid, he proceeds to explain to the prisoner why it is impossible to escape. The person to whom he speaks says nothing and leaves when dismissed. Only one nail clipper remains in the ashtray. The Young Turks of the New Wave who knocked themselves out in the fifties debating the all-important question 'What is cinema?' would've been better off watching Don Siegel films. In *Escape from Alcatraz* the lesson is clear: In the course of one scene the prisoner is established as calculating and taciturn, the warden is shown to be meticulous and self-confident, and we are given a geographic overview of the location. . . ."[2]

This impression (which lasts a full two hours) of getting right to the heart of the matter, we owe to dazzling cutting technique and a finely honed sense of rhythm. As Eastwood remarked: "He (Don) shoots lean and he shoots what he wants. He knew when he had it and he didn't need to cover his ass with a dozen different angles."[3] Both French and American critics underlined the simplicity of the writing, the clarity of style, and the technical perfec-

137

tion. In other words, *Escape from Alcatraz* is a masterpiece of classic filmmaking. Eastwood imparts an undeniable physical and human presence to the remarkably precise unfolding of events. He plays up the mechanical nature of repetitive daily prison routine with considerable skill while at the same time communicating just how little space a prisoner is allotted. Here that's essential, because throughout the film he takes possession of more and more surrounding space.

As for those who accuse Eastwood of having an inexpressive face, the actor replies: "If you look back through history, the people who've been the strongest in film were people who could express a lot by holding certain things in reserve so that the audience is curious to find out what the reserve is. . . . You can see people who think they know what their face is doing because you can see them watching themselves as they're talking to you. If I thought about what my face was doing, I'd really get screwed up. . . . I mean, nobody really knows acting. A lot of things just develop, they stay in your subconscious mind."[4]

1. *Escape from Alcatraz* press kit.
2. *L'Express*, October 27, 1979.
3. *Rolling Stone*, July 4, 1985.
4. *Look*, July 1979.

Bronco Billy

1980

Distribution: Warner-Columbia
Executive Producer: Robert Daley
Producers: Warner/Second Street; Dennis Hackin and Neal Dobrofsky
Associate Producer: Fritz Manes
Director: Clint Eastwood
Assistant Director: Tom Joyner
Second Assistant Directors: Stanley J. Zabka, Richard Graves and Fritz Manes
Screenplay: Dennis Hackin
Director of Photography: David Worth (DeLuxe/Panavision)
Musical Supervision: Snuff Garrett
Music Conducted by: Steve Dorff
Editing: Ferris Webster and Joel Cox
Property Manager: Gene Lourie
Production Manager: Larry Powell
Set Decorator: Ernie Bishop
Set Designer: Jerry MacDonald
Sound Effects Editing: Alan Robert Murray and Bud Asman
Transport: John Reade and Bill Miller
Continuity: Lloyd Nelson

Sound: Bert Hallberg
Rerecording: John T. Reitz
Music Mixing: Grover Helsley
Music Editing: Donald Harris
Cameraman: Jack Green
Assistant cameramen: Leslie Otis and Douglas Olivares
Assistant Set Designer: Lynda Paradise
Electrician: Jack Johnson
Assistant electrician: Sheldon Ehalich
Grips: Don Nygren and John Davis
Special Effects: Jeff Jarvis
Still Photographer: Jack Shannon
Secouriste: James Moffett
Catering: High Noon Mobile Caterers
Makeup: Tom Tuttle
Property Master: Steve Westlund
Costumes: Glenn Wright
Production Secretary: Susan Allen
Accountant: Harry Kohoyda
Secretary to the Producers: Betty Endo
Main Titles and Opticals: Pacific Title
New York Production Coordinator: Manno Productions, Ltd.
Riding Consultant: Alan Cartwright
Lasso Consultant: J. W. Stoker
Length: 116 minutes

With Scatman Crothers

CAST:

Clint Eastwood: *Bronco Billy;* Sondra Locke: *Antoinette Lily;* Geoffrey Lewis: *John Arlington;* Scatman Crothers: *Doc Lynch;* Bill McKinney: *Lefty LeBow;* Sam Bottoms: *Leonard James;* Dan Vadis: *Chief Big Eagle;* Sierra Pecheur: *Lorraine Running Water;* Walter Barnes: *Sheriff Dix;* Woodrow Parfrey: *Dr. Canterbury;* Beverlee McKinsey: *Irene Lily;* Douglas McGrath: *Lieutenant Wiecker;* Hank Worden: *garage man;* William Prince: *Edgar Lipton;* Pam Abbas: *mother superior;* Edye Byrde: *Eloise;* Douglas Copsey: *reporter at bank;* John Wesley Elliott, Jr.: *sanitorium attendant;* Chuck Hicks, Bobby Hoy: *cowboys;* Michael Reinbold: *King;* Tessa Richarde: *Mitzi Fritts;* Tanya Russell: *Doris Duke;* Valerie Shanks: *Sister Maria;* Sharon Sherlock: *license clerk;* James Simmerhan: *bank manager;* Jenny Sternling: *reporter at sanitorium;* Chuck Waters, Jerry Wills: *bank robbers*

Bronco Billy McCoy owns and manages a traveling Wild West show. The motley crew includes Chief Big Eagle, who performs a traditional dance with a rattlesnake, his wife Lorraine Running Water, Leonard "Lasso" James and his rope tricks, Two-Gun Lefty LeBow, Doc Lynch the ringmaster, and Bronco Billy himself, the fastest shot in the West. In need of a female assistant for the routine in which he "liberates" a young lady from a turning wheel with well-placed daggers, Billy hires a snack-bar waitress but wounds her while performing the trick in front of an audience.

At this point in the story enters Antoinette Lily, a rich New York heiress. This product of a spoiled childhood couldn't claim her inheritance until she legally wed, and so she has just married John Arlington, a down-and-out pseudowomanizer. She treats him so badly that he ends up stranding her in their honeymoon hotel in the middle of nowhere. Antoinette meets Bronco Billy at the service station where she's attempting to call for help and Billy manages to hire her despite herself.

Arlington is arrested and accused of having murdered his spouse. At his lawyer's urging he pleads guilty, thinking he'll be shunted off to a psychiatric hospital for three years. He's sentenced to the funny farm for life. In the meantime, Bronco Billy's troupe has troubles of its own. Leonard the lasso king is arrested for having deserted the army. To spring him, Bronco Billy must hand over the troupe's hard-earned savings and accept humiliation before the local sheriff. Then their circus tent burns to the ground. Bronco Billy lays plans to hold up a train, but trains nowadays prove to move a bit too swiftly for that sort of thing. The troupe shows up to give their annual free show at the insane asylum where Arlington is incarcerated. Arlington recognizes Antoinette. She returns to New York to testify and to put her affairs in order. But she misses the circus. One night, Bronco Billy sees her reappear in the arena under the Big Top . . .

Bronco Billy, Eastwood's seventh directorial effort, was shot in Idaho, Oregon, and New York. It was, up until the making of *Honkytonk Man,* Eastwood's favorite among his films and the most revealing of his true personality. "It was an old-fashioned theme," he would later say. "Probably too old-fashioned since the film didn't do as well as we hoped. But if, as a film director, I ever wanted to say something, you'll find it in *Bronco Billy.*"[1]

This "something" had already been touched upon in *Breezy* and *The Outlaw Josey Wales,* both of which praised individualism in the face of "the Establishment." Moreover, Bronco Billy and his troupe, flotsam and jetsam of the American dream, are direct descendants of the hippie commune in *Josey Wales.* And paradoxically, it is they who reinvent the American dream by completely separating it from social and material success. As French critic Alain Garel sums things up: "This whole world unto itself peopled with criminals and dissidents, this 'melting pot' of ethnic and social minorities, lives in a spirit of loyalty, camaraderie, self-sacrifice, and a total absence of material preoccupations. That is to say that aside from their individual personalities which set them apart, they lose status in society's eyes by virtue of their lifestyle. And yet, compared to society—which in this case consists exclusively of rotten hateful sheriffs, unnerving asylum directors, crooked lawyers, inconsolable widows, dowry-chasing gigolos, and all the criminals who, take note, manufacture American flags—these 'abnormal' people appear to be extraordinarily sane. Rather than be (or appear to be) products of this society, they are what they want to be as recommended by Bronco Billy, himself a creation of his own resolve."[2]

In reality Bronco Billy is an urban shoe salesman turned "mythic figure of the West," acting out his love for the Western, fueled by pop culture, both filmic and literary. Chief Big Eagle and his faithful squaw are actually two caucasians who always dreamed of being Indians (Big Eagle is constantly being bitten by the snakes he claims to master). All the rest of the troupe is made up of petty criminals who have served their time and paid their debt to society. And having "paid," they've all decided to be someone other than who their government files say they are—a jovial and radical means of taking issue with society without resorting to violence.

Through his portrayal of Bronco Billy, Eastwood has a good time further demolishing his trademark screen persona (or what's left of it). He's an unfailingly accurate sharpshooter who wounds his assistant. As a Western bandit he tries to attack a train

With Edye Byrde

barrelling down the track faster than any horse could hope to gallop. As a man of liberal principles, he chastises any troupe member who makes a suggestion or takes the initiative. Gallant and courteous, he throws a fit when his assistant changes a word in her prepared speech. Macho, he lets the woman he loves lead him around by the nose. And finally, though he may be the "fastest shot in the West" under the big top, he accepts humiliation of his marksmanship by a boastful sheriff in order to free Leonard, a Vietnam deserter. And this in spite of his fierce patriotism.

This time America got the message loud and clear and the film drew quasi-glowing reviews. *Variety* admitted that Eastwood was gifted for comedy, the *New York Daily News* praised his skill with the "slow burn," and the *New York Post* admired his unpretentiousness. And finally, in the *Village Voice,* bastion of the intellectual left, Tom Allen wrote, "Now it's time to take him seriously, not only as a popular phenomenon, but as one of the most honest and influential movie personalities of our time."[3]

The French critical establishment responded somewhat differently to this "ballad of misfits." Giles Colpart saw it as "sure enough the product of a vigilante America."[4] Robert Chazal pointed out that "Clint Eastwood, who often addresses himself to children, takes this occasion to celebrate friendship, discipline, faith in hard work, and patriotism."[5] Jean de Baroncelli wants to know whether the words pitched to the kids in the audience are spoken by Clint Eastwood "or a candidate named Reagan."[6] And as for critic Pierre Murat, he concludes that "Bronco Billy wants to be (or presumes to be) America as she likes to be thought of, healthy and happy. 'Now listen up all you little pards,' Bronco Billy proclaims to his young audience which listens rapt and

filled with wonder. 'Eat your breakfast, don't lie, and obey your parents'. . . . One couldn't possibly be more clear.''[7] First of all, the speech is bent somewhat out of shape by Mr. Murat. And secondly, the critic is forgetting one essential feature of Bronco Billy's pep talk, the kindly admonition ''Don't forget to say your prayers.''

Finally, as in the United States, Eastwood would be defended by the intellectual left. The popular daily paper *Libération* was sorry to see a film which was ''terrifically interesting, well directed, where the action unfolds on many levels,'' do poorly at the box office.[8] And Phillipe Garnier hit the nail on the head, writing: ''There's a touch of Capra (just as irresistible and just as embarrassing) in the air in *Bronco Billy*. It's the story of a man who follows as far as his dream will take him, not deluding himself, but in the spirit of 'What if?' It's a little bit like *It's a Wonderful Life* without flashbacks or a guardian angel. Thanks to his offbeat brand of obstinacy, a full army of social misfits and spiritually wounded have a roof over their heads—the big top.''[9]

P.S. Clint Eastwood sings a duet with country-western great Merle Haggard, and four additional songs accompany the story.

1. ''Etoiles et Toiles'' (television broadcast), France, December 1982.
2. *La Revue du Cinéma*, no. 354, October 1980.
3. *Village Voice*, June 16, 1980.
4. *La Saison Cinématographique*, 1981.
5. *France-Soir*, September 11, 1980.
6. *Le Monde*, September 12, 1980.
7. *Télérama*, September 13, 1980.
8. *Libération*, October 8, 1980.
9. *Rock and Folk*, no. 172, May 1981.

Any Which Way You Can

1981

Distribution: Warner
Producer: Warner/Malpaso; Fritz Manes
Executive Producer: Robert Daley
Production Attaché: William J. Creber
Production Manager: Larry Powell
Director: Buddy Van Horn
Assistant Director: Tom Joyner
Second Assistant Directors: Stan Zabka, David Valdes and Fritz Manes
Screenplay: Stanford Sherman
Musical Supervision: Steve Dorf and Snuff Garrett
Director of Photography: David Worth
Editing: Ferris Webster and Ron Spang
Set Design: Ernie Bishop
Property Manager: Jerry MacDonald
Script Supervisor: Lloyd Nelson
Sound Effects Editing: Alan Robert Murray and Bob Asman
Production Managers: John Reade and Bill Miller
Sound: Bert Halberg
Sound Mixing: Vern Poore and Grover Helsley
Sound Editing: Donald Harris
Assistant Editor: Jud Nealon

Camera Operator: Jack Green and Douglas Ryan
Assistant Camera Operators: Leslie Otis, Douglas Olivares, Steve Tate and Marco Koiwa
Key Grip: Jack Johnson
Special Effects: Chuck Gaspar and Jeff Jarvis
Still Photographer: Jack Shannon
Costumes: Glenn Wright
Length: 116 minutes

CAST:

Clint Eastwood: *Philo Beddoe;* Sondra Locke: *Lynn Halsey-Taylor;* Geoffrey Lewis: *Orville;* William Smith: *Jack Wilson;* Harry Guardino: *James Beekman;* Ruth Gordon: *Ma;* Michael Cavanaugh: *Patrick Scarfe;* Barry Corbin: *Fat Zack;* Roy Jenson: *Moody;* Bill McKinney: *Dallas;* Dan Vadis: *Frank;* Glen Campbell: *Glen Campbell;* William O'Connell: *Elmo;* John Quade: *Cholla;* Al Ruscio; Camila Ashlend; Julie Brown; Johnny Duncan; Michael Fairman; James Gaunnon; Lynn Hallowell; Ken Lerner; George Murdock; Jack Murdock; Ann Nelson; Kent Perkins; Tessa Richarde; Anne Ramsey; Jim Stafford; Michael Talbott; Mark Taylor; Jack Tibean

Philo Beddoe takes on the ''king of the cops'' in a fistfight on the side of the road before an audience of truckers who have broadcast word of the match via

CB radio. Philo emerges victorious but informs Orville that his fighting days are over. Meanwhile, in a luxurious hotel on the East Coast, James Beekman, professional gambler and Mafia member, pits a snake against a mongoose for very high stakes. After this slightly peculiar fight, Beekman and his associate talk over the possibility of organizing a historic bout between Philo and a certain Jack Smith, undefeated in the East.

Philo, Orville, and their orangutan Clyde go into a bar for a beer. Philo's old girlfriend Lynn happens to be singing there. She wants to win Philo back and does so in record time. On the other hand, a band of low-rent Hell's Angels, the Black Widows, are still trying to torment the life out of Philo. One of Beekman's men contacts Philo and offers him $25,000 to fight Wilson. Philo accepts and takes care of his problem with Lynn by taking her away from her rooming house for single women and having her move in with him.

While in training, Philo meets Wilson and hits it off with him. Philo saves Wilson from a near-fatal fall and, that same night, Wilson rescues Philo from a knife attack. The two men are even; Wilson no longer wants to fight against Philo. Egged on by Lynn and Orville, Philo also backs down. But Beekman doesn't see things that way.

Philo treats Lynn and Clyde to a little excursion. He "borrows" a female orangutan from the zoo and everyone heads for a motel. In the meantime, armed bullies show up at Philo's place, rough up Orville, and get Ma to reveal the address of the motel. But Ma heads off after them, along with Orville, and the resulting uproar at the motel is such that the mafiosi don't stand a chance. Amid the hullabaloo Ma seduces the night watchman.

In the process of returning the ape to the zoo, Philo and Lynn are attacked by Beekman's men and Lynn is kidnapped. Under the circumstances Philo agrees to the fight. Once Wilson hears what's up he finds out where Lynn is and sets out to the rescue along with Philo and Orville. Orville is wounded in the ensuing battle. Passing for a hero, Orville seduces his nurse.

Wilson and Philo officially cancel the fight, but can't resist finding out which of them really is the better man. They fight each other in private. They're spotted in the act by a bunch of kids, then by a cop who lets his buddies in on the secret. Pretty soon the whole town stampedes to watch. Seeing which way the fight is going, Beekman orders his men to kill Philo. The motorcycle hoodlums have placed their bets on Philo and so find it expedient to save his life. When the match is over Philo sports a broken arm, but is the winner all the same. He and Wilson part good friends.

As a sequel to *Every Which Way But Loose, Any Which Way You Can* stands apart from its predecessor in two ways. For one thing, the protagonists are looked upon more kindly. Philo is more sensitive to romance, Orville is less selfish, and even old Ma finds the strength to hit the road if it means saving one of her "kids." Ma also gives in to one last sexual escapade. The humor is more resolutely grounded in the wacky and absurd. The motorcycle gang behaves like the Monty Python crew, the orangutan defecates in police cars, and everyone has only one goal in mind: to get laid and have a ball.

Alas, apart from the first nonchalant half hour, which takes place in country music bars, *Any Which Way You Can* is scarcely any better than *Every Which Way But Loose*. The humor falls short and turns to gross farce, the scenes are overdone, and the urge to make fun of the Mafia is just as demagogic as was the desire to make the cops and the motorcycle gang look ridiculous in the first episode. So allow us to express our surprise at the reaction of Christian Bosséno who, after having defended James Fargo's film, finds that in the sequel "the imagery leads to nausea" and that "Clint Eastwood, in whom certain among us had seriously believed, has deliberately decided to take the demagogic and 'profitable' path, that of shamelessly exploiting one of the very lowest strains of American humor."[1] It's interesting to note that he's neglected to give this same Eastwood "in whom certain among us had believed" credit for *Bronco Billy,* made just before and, what's more, written up in that very same issue of *La Saison Cinématographique.* Maybe *Bronco Billy,* in retrospect, would justify the hopes that "certain" people had held? But it makes little difference—we have here yet another sterling example of selective memory.

Shot in the summer of 1980, *Any Which Way You Can* was released nationwide that Christmas and did quite well. In conclusion, let us also note that here once again Eastwood gave a break to a young director—in this case to Buddy Van Horn, who had served as second unit director on several of Eastwood's preceding films. Eastwood marked his own return to the realm of song by singing the title duet with Ray Charles.

---

1. *La Saison Cinématographique,* 1981.

Firefox

1982

Distribution: Warner-Columbia
Producer: Warner/Malpaso
Associate Producer: Paul Hitchcock
Executive Producer: Fritz Manes
Production Managers: Steve Perry and Fritz Manes
Director: Clint Eastwood
First Assistant Director: Steve Perry
Second Assistant Director: David Valdes
Screenplay: Alex Lasker, Wendell Wellman, based on the novel by Craig Thomas
Director of Photography: Bruce Surtees (Panavision)
Art Directors: John Graysmark and Elayne Ceder
Editing: Ferris Webster and Ron Spang
Music: Donald Harris
Original Music Composed by: Maurice Jarre
Casting: Marion Dougherty and Mary Selway
Set Design: Ernie Bishop
Sound Effects: Alan Robert Murray and Bud Asman
Sound Effect Editor: Bob Henderson
Continuity: Lloyd Nelson
Sound Mixing: Don Johnson, Les Fresholtz
Key Grip: Jules Strasser
Camera Operator: Jack Green
Assistant Cameramen: Mike Weldon and Jeff Miller
Set Manager: Joe Acord
Gaffers: Charles Saldana, Bruce Spellman
Electrician: Don Nygren
Special Effects: Chuck Gaspar
Still Photographer: Jack Shannon
Negative Cutter: Jack Hooper
Costume Supervisor: Glenn Wright
Property Manager: Edward Aiona
Makeup: Christina Smith
Production Secretary: Linda Sony
Production Assistant: Betty Endo
Special Effects Producer: John Dykstra
Special Effects Supervisor: Robert Shepherd
Scientific Consultants: Durk Pearson and Sandy Shaw, Dr. Jack Wheeler

European Crew:
Production Manager: Dieter Meyer
Production Coordinator: Ilse Schwarzwald
Assistant Directors: Don French and Charles Furth
Casting (Australia): Renata Arbes
Assistant Art Director: Thomas Riccabona
Designer: Alan Tomkins
Costumes: Bert Hearn and Hans Ziegelwagner
Camera Assistants: Ronald B. Hersey and Moritz Gieselman
Gaffer: Dennis Fraser
Electrician: Erich Kristusek

Special Effects: Karl Baumgarnter
Assistant Editor: David Hitchcock
Costumes: Waltraut Freitag and Ille Sievers
Length: 124 minutes

CAST:
Clint Eastwood: *Mitchell Gant;* Freddie Jones: *Kenneth Aubrey;* David Huffman: *Buckholz;* Warren Clarke: *Pavel Upenskoy;* Ronald Lacey: *Semelovsky;* Kenneth Colley: *Colonel Kontarsky;* Klaus Lowitsch: *General Vladimirov;* Nigel Hawthorne: *Pyotr Baranovitch;* Stefan Schnabel: *First Secretary;* Thomas Hill: *General Brown;* Clive Merrison: *Major Lanyev;* Kai Wulff: *Lieutenant Voskov;* Dimitra Arliss: *Natalia;* Austin Willis: *Walters;* Michael Currie: *Captain Seerbacker;* James Staley: *Lieutenant Commander Fleischer;* Ward Costello: *General Rogers;* Alan Tilvern: *Air Marshal Kutuzov;* Oliver Cotton: *Dimitri Priabin;* Bernard Behrens: *William Saltonstall;* Richard Derr: *Admiral Curtin;* Woody Eney: *Major Dietz;* Bernard Erhard: *KGB guard;* Hugh Fraser: *Police Inspector Tortyev;* David Gant: *KGB official;* John Grillo: *customs*

officer; Czeslaw Grocholski: *Old man;* Barrie Houghton: *Boris Glazunov;* Neil Hunt: *Richard Cunningham;* Vincent J. Isaacs: *radio operator;* Alexei Jawdokimov: *radio cryptographer;* Wolf Kahler: *Andropov, KGB director;* Eugene Lipinski: *KGB agent;* Phillip Littell: *radio cryptographer;* Curt Lowens: *Dr Schuller;* Lev Mailer: *Shower guard;* Fritz Manes: *captain;* David Meyers: *Grosch;* Alfredo Michelson: *interrogator;* Zenno Nahayevsky: *air officer;* Georges Orrison: *Leon Sprague;* Tony Papenfuss, Grisha Plotkin: *GRU officers;* Olivier Pierre: *Borkh;* George Pravda: *General Borov;* John Ratzen-Berger: *Peck;* Alex Rodine: *Captain of Riga;* Lance Rosen: *agent;* Eugene Scherer: *Russian captain;* Warrick Sims: *Shelley;* Mike Spero: *Russian guard;* Malcolm Storry: *KGB agent;* Chris Winfield: *RAF operator;* John Yates: *Admiral Pearson;* Alexander Zale: *launch controller;* Igor Zatsepin: *flight engineer;* Konstantin Zlatev: *technician*

Soviet researchers working in absolute secrecy in military laboratories have perfected an incredibly fearsome fighter plane, the Firefox. Without a competitor in sight, the apparatus truly qualifies as the "ultimate weapon." It travels at six times the speed of sound, it is invisible to radar, and—it's most revolutionary feature—the nuclear missiles on board are fired through the pilot's thought commands. The Western world's secret services meet in special session and decide to implement "Operation Firefox," whereby an American pilot will be smuggled into East Germany in order to steal the plane. The man chosen for the job is Major Mitchell Gant, a semiretired elite pilot. Gant, seriously affected by his experiences in Vietnam, is obsessed with the memory of a burning village and seems to have lost his nerve. He's put through an intensive simulated flight training program to hone his reflexes.

Posing as an American black-marketeer, Gant enters East Germany and is taken under the wing of a group of dissidents working for the internal resistance. A man is murdered right in front of his eyes, Gant is given a new identity, and blends into anonymity. The KGB, well aware of Gant's presence in the country, mobilizes to locate him. Gant narrowly escapes an identity check in the subway. The close call, which entails a policeman's death, is traumatic, and Gant feels raw fear begin to take hold. Finally, a Jewish dissident scientist named Semelovsky, who works on the Firefox, gets Gant onto the base disguised as an air force officer. Semelovsky and his friends try to immobilize the second Firefox prototype in order to create a sufficient diversion so that Gant can steal the plane and also be assured that he won't be followed. They die trying, but Gant

manages to get on board and take off. He heads due North. After a refueling stop in an ice field Gant sets off for the Free World. Suddenly the second Firefox, piloted by the top flying ace in the Soviet air force, looms behind Gant in the sky. A titanic duel begins.

The relative failure of *Bronco Billy* had left Eastwood in a *"mal paso."* At the very least it proved that it wasn't the subtle messages of *Josey Wales* or *The Gauntlet* that packed in his customary audience, but rather the image played up in advertisements of an invincible adventurer, revolvers in hand, or of one man alone against all, next to a bullet-ridden bus with a beautiful young woman at his side. These images promised violence in the tradition of Dirty Harry, a character so popular with fans that his third adventure, *The Enforcer,* despite being the most mediocre of the three, ranks as Eastwood's second-biggest-grossing film (behind *Every Which Way But Loose*). Apparently the audience for these films didn't go out of its way to see *Bronco Billy,* which was quickly catalogued as a "kid's movie." And the hoped-for "new" audience behaved as usual; people with a preconceived notion of Clint Eastwood movies weren't about to attend a Clint Eastwood movie.

Firefox came about due to these circumstances. The actor had to find another invincible hero to portray in an action-packed context. Eastwood set his sights on a best-selling novel by Craig Thomas which, in Eastwood's opinion, featured situations which would lend themselves to agonizing suspense and spectacular effects. His choice was probably the right one, since *Firefox* placed twelfth among the biggest-grossing films released in the United States in 1982. Although the film is far from his best, it remains of interest due to the reactions it provoked, the character Eastwood portrays, and the audience targeted by the director.

Without getting too wrapped up in polemics, keep in mind that *Firefox* was interpreted in radically different ways by French and American critics. To simplify matters, let's just say that the reviewers split up into two camps: those who took the film seriously and those who took it primarily as a comedy.

Jacques Zimmer, a critic who had formerly defended Eastwood, asserted that "If *Bronco Billy* managed to maintain the illusion of self-parody one has to say straight out that *Firefox* is idiocy incarnate and easily oversteps the boundaries of involuntary humor. . . . *Firefox* boasts a deadpan seriousness compounded by a disconcerting aura of conviction. And the joke sort of congeals around the depiction of a communist world peopled by the worst caricatures imaginable."[1] For French critic Robert Chazal, who otherwise defends Eastwood, "It's with films like this that the idea is kept alive for the general public of the balance which is essential between the military forces of East and West."[2] Jacques Siclier qualifies

the matter with: "Clint Eastwood shows international espionage services to be organizations which behave coldly and cynically in the rivalry for military supremacy between the superpowers. The Russian dissidents are sacrificed as cavalierly by the agents from the West as they are by the KGB." None of this prevents Eastwood from having "the current ideology of the star-spangled banner emerge triumphant."[3]

Gérard Lefort of *Libération* takes an entirely different approach: "And what if *Firefox* were a comedy? Well then, split your sides at the outlandish view of Soviet manners, laugh yourself hoarse over the wretched comrade first secretary whose first reflex after the Firefox is stolen is to ask Eastwood by radio if he would be so kind as to give back 'something which doesn't belong to him,' and lose any remaining vestiges of self-control over the scene where, landing in an ice field for a refueling rendezvous with a U.S. submarine, Clint's first words, fresh out of the cockpit, are a request that someone 'check the oil and tire pressure.' A sufficient number of narrow escapes confirms that, like all great come-

dians, beneath Clint Eastwood's unruffled countenance lurks an irresistible urge to grin."[4]

There's no question that humor exists in *Firefox,* most notably in the scenes cited by Gérard Lefort. But the character played by Eastwood is not intended as parody—far from it. Nor does he fit into the tradition of "Yankee heroes of legendary courage."[2] He is quite the opposite—"a worn-out hero, mentally destroyed, who seems to want to buy off his bad conscience."[3] This is incontestably the most interesting aspect of *Firefox.* Eastwood is fifty years old and will not, or cannot, go on playing imperturbable heroes. His elite fighter pilot is physically drained, obsessed by the Vietnam war and the part he played in its massacres (fairly surprising for a film that's allegedly simple-minded and anticommunist), can't stand violence and gives in to fear whenever it rears its head, is obliged to pose as a black-market businessman, to lie, to steal, and even to kill. In other words, we are miles removed from the Eastwood prototype as defined by Don Siegel; *He is no longer in control of the situation.* As for the anti-Soviet angle, it's somewhat paradoxical to see the most powerful nation in the world, the U.S.A. obliged to send a man to steal a prototype and in so doing acknowledge that its enemy possesses an enormous technological advantage. As for the state of American vigilance vis-à-vis Soviet weaponry, that's nothing new. The film only makes use of the given state of affairs.

All of which brings us to the audience *Firefox* is aimed at. Does the film merit the raising of such lofty questions? I would say not. The idea that Eastwood is a reactionary is so deeply embedded in the collective critical spirit that it can be pushed forward at the slightest pretext without anyone feeling the need to take preceding films into account. Eastwood made his position on *Firefox* sufficiently clear during an interview for a French television show devoted to cinema, *Etoiles et Toiles*.[5] He is, above all, an entertainer who needed an action-packed vechicle. From this perspective, the nature of the film's flaws become significant. Working casually, as he sometimes does, Eastwood shot his script without trying to fill in all the gaps or avoid all the inconsistencies. You can't make me believe that the man behind *Josey Wales,* so attentive to detail, so careful to establish the authenticity of the most minor costume in his only historical film, was unaware of enormous discrepancies—such as the fact that the Russian authorities speak among themselves in English while the cop on the beat speaks Russian, or that the pilot steals the ultrasecret prototype without difficulty, etc.

As an entertainer Eastwood is tackling yet another popular category of adventure film: After the thriller and the Western, he's trying his hand at espionage. He's not looking for seamless credibility so much as for efficient storytelling and plenty of action. The most surprising thing, without a doubt, is that the only "serious" point of view in the film is moral: The vile conduct of the secret agencies and the wholesale sacrifice of dissidents bring to mind Alfred Hitchcock's *Torn Curtain,* in which another American enters Russia to steal a secret formula, at whatever cost.

The first three-quarters of *Firefox* is there only to lead up to the stunning bravura of the final thirty minutes. When the two prototypes enter into their duel in the skies, John Dykstra's special effects openly invite comparison with *Star Wars.* And suddenly the strategy of *Firefox* becomes clear. Eastwood at first carries on in the tradition which shot him to stardom, then ventures into the most popular realm of the contemporary, cinema, the domain of electronic wizardry. He's out to win back "his" public, but also aims to win over a younger crowd. He doesn't entirely succeed, due to a lack of conviction. *Firefox,* a transitional film, lacks heart. That heart is present and accounted for in *Honkytonk Man.*

1. *La Revue du Cinéma,* no. 377, November 1982.
2. *France-Soir,* December 20, 1982.
3. *Le Monde,* December 25, 1982.
4. *Libération,* December 20, 1982.
5. *Etoiles et Toiles,* (French TV broadcast), December 1982.

With Bruce Surtees

Honkytonk Man

1982

Distribution: Warner
Producer: Warner/Malpast; Clint Eastwood
Executive Producer: Fritz Manes
Director: Clint Eastwood
First Assistant Director: Tony Brown
Second Assistant Director: Tom Seidman
Screenplay based on his novel: Clancy Carlile
Director of Photography: Bruce Surtees (Technicolor/Panavision)
Art Director: Edward Carfagno
Editors: Ferris Webster, Michael Kelly, and Joel Cox
Music Conducted by: Steve Dorff
Musical Supervision: Snuff Garrett
Production Manager: Steve Perry
Casting: Phyllis Huffman and Susan Arnold
Set Designer: Gary Moreno
Sound Editors: Alan Robert Murray, Bob Henderson, and Bud Asman
Continuity: Lloyd Nelson
Sound Mixing: Don Johnson
Rerecording Mixer: John Reitz, David Campbell, and Joe Citarella
Camera Operator: Jack Green
Assistant Camera Operators: Leo Napolitano and Marc Margulis
Supervising Set Designer: Michael Muscarella
Head Gaffer: Charles Saldana
Gaffers: Bruce Spellman and Kirk E. Bales
Head Electrician: Tom Stern
Special Effects: Wayne Edgar
Still Photographer: Michael Middleton
Publicity: Marco Barla
Costumes: Glenn Wright, Aida Swinson
Properties: Addie Aiona
Makeup: David Dittmar
Hairdresser: Marlene Williams
Production Secretary: Linda Sony
Length: 122 minutes

CAST:

Clint Eastwood: *Red Stovall;* Kyle Eastwood: *Whit;* John McIntire: *Grandpa;* Alexa Kenin: *Marlene;* Verna Bloom: *Emmy;* Matt Clark: *Arnspriger;* Jerry Hardin: *Snuffy;* Tim Thomerson: *highway patrolman;* Macon McCalman: *Dr. Hines;* Joe Regalbuto: *Henry Axle;* Gary Grubbs: *Jim Bob;* Rebecca Clemons: *Belle;* John Gimble: *Bob Wills;* Linda Hopkins: *Flossie;* Betty Ford: *Lulu;* Jim Boelsen: *Junior;* Tracey Walter: *Pooch;* Susan Peretz: *Miss Maud;* John Russell: *Jack Wade;* Charles Cyphers: *Stubbs;* Marty Robbins: *Smoky;* Ray Price: *Bob Wills singer;* Shelley West, David Frizzell: *singers at Grand Ole Opry;* Porter Wagoner: *Dusty;* Bob Ferrera: *eldest son;* Tracy Shults: *the girl;* R. J. Ganzert: *the rancher;* Hugh Warden: *grocer;* Kelsie Blades: *veteran;* Jim Ahart: *waiter;* Steve Autry: *mechanic;* Peter Griggs: *Mr. Vogel;* Julie Hoopman: *prostitute;* Rozelle Gayle: *club manager;* Robert V. Barron, DeForest Covan: *grave diggers;* Lloyd Nelson: *disc jockey;* George Orrison: *jailbird;* Glenn Wright: *jailbird;* Frank Reinhard: *stand-in;* Roy Jenson: *Dub;* Sherry Allurd: *Dub's wife;* Gordon Terry, Tommy Alsup, Merle Travis: *the Texas Playboys;* Robert D. Carver, Thomas Powels: *bus drivers*

The story takes place in the early thirties, during the Great Depression. Red Stovall, an itinerant musician with a special fondness for women and strong drink, earns his living by performing in roadhouses. On his way to Nashville for an audition at the Grand Ole Opry, Red stops at the miserable Oklahoma farm where his sister Emmy and her husband are struggling to make ends meet. Red's arrival during a duststorm is rather dramatic. Dead drunk, he plows

John McIntire

Kyle Eastwood

through the gate with his beat-up old car. His only luggage is his guitar. Emmy knows that Red is ill and irresponsible and so gives her fourteen-year-old son Whit permission to accompany Uncle Red to Nashville. Whit will drive the car and keep his uncle ''out of trouble.'' Grandpa also comes along for the ride since he wants to return to his native Tennessee, which he hasn't seen for forty-five years, to spend his final years.

Red, Whit, and Grandpa encounter numerous adventures along the way. Red is attacked by an angry bull while bathing in an outdoor tub, Whit gets his first taste of romance in the arms of a young prostitute, and Grandpa rediscovers the site of the heady rush for virgin territory he took part in as a young man in the unspoiled West. While trying to collect an old debt, Red finds himself mixed up in an attempted holdup and the trio inherits Marlene, a high-strung young woman who dreams of being a great singer but sings way off key. From inn to tavern, from brothel to jazz club, Whit discovers the wandering life and learns to understand his uncle. Finally the ''quartet'' find themselves with car trouble in some two-bit town in the middle of nowhere. Grandpa goes his own way and Red hops a bus bound for Nashville, suggesting to Whit that he find a way to ditch Marlene.

Red passes his audition at the Grand Ole Opry but a coughing fit stops him from finishing his song. The doctor informs Whit that his uncle has tuberculosis and doesn't have long to live. Although his strength has almost entirely given out, Red agrees to make a record, the last chance he'll ever have ''to be somebody.'' A short time later he dies with Whit and Marlene (who managed to find them again) at his bedside. The two adolescents are the only people present at Red's burial. As they make their way from the cemetery a car goes by and the song on its radio is Red's ''Honkytonk Man.''

Clint Eastwood chose to be a honkytonk man strumming his way from roadhouse to roadhouse, off the beaten path and on the open road, in his ninth directorial effort. Red Stovall is a guy outside the system, close to Bronco Billy in spirit. The third novel of country-western composer and singer Clancy Carlile (whom Eastwood also hired to adapt his own work for the screen) was the basis for the project.

One needn't have a crystal ball to see why Eastwood was drawn to a story which takes three generations into account against the backdrop of the Depression. Eastwood was born in 1930, smack dab

With Alexa Kenin

in the middle of the prevailing economic crisis. The poverty and transience the film describes stem from his own childhood. There is an obvious desire on the director's part to get back to his roots and, much as with *Josey Wales,* to pay tribute to a culture and heritage which is uniquely American.

Red Stovall, "honkytonk man," is the sort of character Eastwood is fond of. He's an individualist with a soft spot for alcohol and women, determined to get his little piece of the American dream. Red shows up at his sister's Oklahoma farm with nothing but his old Lincoln, his guitar, and the shirt on his back, but he seems to have more than his sister and his brother-in-law, whose orderly life on their orderly failing farm is a study in misery.

In a remarkable introduction, Eastwood introduces his characters without passing judgment on their chosen lifestyles. Poverty evens things out to a certain extent, but for these folks, the "American dream" is in no way synonymous with material success. In Bronco Billy fashion, Red wants to *live* the American dream. Bronco Billy wanted to be a cowboy, Red wants to sing at the Grand Ole Opry. But Eastwood goes farther than he did in *Bronco Billy* by teaming Red with an adolescent and an old man who will serve as sources of enlightenment in the course of the journey.

Grandpa represents America's past. In one of the film's finest scenes, veteran actor John McIntire (who worked with Anthony Mann, Raoul Walsh, and Jacques Tourneur in the fifties and here makes a noted comeback) brings to life the land rush of his youth for Kyle Eastwood (who plays his grandson). His vivid memories are all the more bittersweet because they hark back to a time when everything seemed possible, and he is speaking of them at a time when the Depression has shot down a great many hopes and dreams. But Grandpa isn't complaining, just reminiscing. "Did you get some of the land?" asks his grandson.

"I got mine. I lost it later. That doesn't matter. It was not just the land. It was the dream. We were dream chasers," he replies before scooping up a bit of earth in his hands, concluding, "Look at it now. It all turned to dust." Won, then lost—no big deal, no harm done. This is Red's basic philosophy as well. Red lives hard, burning the candle at both ends, bouncing from honkytonk to brothel, sleeping in fleabag hotels, getting saddled with a slightly hysterical young woman and succumbing to tuberculosis, having managed to make a record just in the nick of time. He too has no complaints. His only regret is doubtless having botched the great love of his life. But life on the road provides; the trick is to have a direction to go in. Young Whit, played by Eastwood's own son, learns about life through his uncle and helps Red get in touch with himself at the same time. Without Whit we wouldn't know of Red's loneliness, his tenderness, his occasional regret. Whit's "education" comes to pass in the sorts of places where youngsters aren't usually allowed. But those same places are apparently where real human beings mingle and Whit's rites of passage occur in a joyous atmosphere. Whit, who has heard his parents complain all his life, finds his grandfather's philosophy at work among Red's cronies: win some, lose some, here today, gone tomorrow.

Honkytonk Man was shot entirely on location in Sacramento, in the Sonora region of Northern Cal-

159

With Bob Ferrera, John McIntire, Verna Bloom, Tracy Shults, and Matt Clark

ifornia, in Carson City, Nevada, and in Nashville, Tennessee. "Shooting on location keeps you in touch with reality," says Eastwood, who reaffirms his faith in small crews and quick shoots. "It's easier that way because the crew gets into the spirit of a film when it's working far away from studio soundstages. I choose my crew as carefully as I do my actors. I think that's why I've always had technicians who do a great job. When we move we do it together and we never stay in the same spot too long. I like to keep a rhythm going. I don't think I could work slowly if I tried."[1]

In the style of *Every Which Way But Loose,* *Bronco Billy,* and *Any Which Way You Can,* the soundtrack of *Honkytonk Man* is particularly rich and features a number of country-western songs, including several performed by Eastwood himself.

Despite one or two slow passages, *Honkytonk Man* is, to this day, Eastwood's most accomplished film.

It includes what are perhaps the finest scenes he's shot: John McIntire's evocation of the rush to claim new land, and the recording session for the final song, interrupted by a violent coughing fit. Red Stovall is a tragic brother to Bronco Billy because he dies at the end calling the name of the sweetheart he abandoned in his youth. But all the same, Eastwood doesn't give in to sentimentality, as Richard Schickel clearly saw: "If there are any people left who doubt Eastwood's accomplishments as a screen actor, they had better come around for this lesson in underplaying a long, strong scene. In a season when everyone suffers the tyranny of the sentimental, one feels a special gratitude for people who do not know the meaning of the word cute."[2]

---

1. American press kit for *Honkytonk Man.*
2. *Time,* December 20, 1982.

160

Sudden Impact

1983

Distribution: Warner
Producer: Clint Eastwood
Director: Clint Eastwood
Screenplay: Joseph C. Stinson, after an original story by Earl E. Smith and Charles B. Pierce, based on the characters created by Harry Julian Fink and Rita M. Fink
Unit Production Manager: Fritz Manes
Director of Photography: Bruce Surtees (Technicolor/Panavision)
Art Director: Edward Carfango
Editor: Joel Cox
Music: Lalo Schifrin
Production Manager: Steve Perry
First Assistant Director: David Valdes
Second Assistant Director: Paul Moen
Associate Producer: Steve Perry
Casting: Marion Dougherty
Set Decoration: Ernie Bishop
Sound Effects Editors: Alan Robert Murray, Bob Henderson, and Bob Asman
Music Editor: Donald Harris
Continuity: Lloyd Nelson
Assistant Editor: John Morrisey
Sound Engineer: Don Johnson
Grip: Jules Strasser
Camera Operator: Jack Green
Assistant Cameramen: John Walker and Jeff Miller
Stunt Coordinator: Wayne Van Horn
Gaffer: Bruce Spellman
Head Electrician: Tom Stern
Assistant Electrician: Ed Ayer
Special Effects: Chuck Gaspar
Still Photographer: Marsha Reed
Dresser: Darryl Athons
Makeup: Barbara Guedell
Production Secretary: Linda Sony
Secretary to the Producers: Judie Hoyt
Production Assistant: Jim Porter
Set Designer: Bob Lawless
Length: 117 minutes

CAST:

Clint Eastwood: *Harry Callahan;* Sondra Locke: *Jennifer Spencer;* Pat Hingle: *Jannings;* Bradford Dillman: *Captain Briggs;* Paul Drake: *Mick;* Audrie J. Neenan: *Ray Parkins;* Jack Thibeau: *Kruger;* Michael Currie: *Lieutenant Donnelly;* Albert Popwell: *Horace King;* Mark Keyloun: *Bennett;* Kevyn Major Howard: *Hawkins;* Bette Ford: *Leah;* Nancy Parsons: *Mrs. Kruger;* Joe Bellan: *Detective Burly;* Wendell Wellman: *Tyrone;* Mara Corday: *waitress;* Russ McCubbin: *Eddie;* Robert Sutton: *Carl;* Carmen Ar-genziano: *D'Ambrosia;* Lisa Britt: *Elizabeth;* Bill Reddick: *Police Chief;* Lois DeBanzie: *judge;* Matthew Child: *Alby;* Michael Johnson, Nick Dimitri: *Killers;* Michael Maurer: *George Wilburn;* Pat Duval: *Bailiff;* Christian Phillips, Steven Kravitz: *Hawkins's buddies;* Dennis Royston, Melvin Thompson, Jophery Brown, Bill Upton: *young people;* Christopher Pray: *Detective Jacobs;* James McEachin: *Detective Barnes;* Maria Lynch: *hostess;* Ken Lee: *Loomis;* Morgan Upton: *bartender;* John X. Heart: *uniformed policeman;* David Gonzales, Albert Martinez, David Rivers, Robert Rivers: *gang members;* Harry Demopopoulos: *Dr. Barton;* Lisa London: *young prostitute;* Tom Spratley: *old man;* Eileen Wiggins: *hysterical customer;* John Novak: *bank robber*

Dawn in San Francisco. A couple is necking in a car parked atop a cliff. Suddenly, the young woman

pleased by the arrival of this urban cop—particularly in view of the fact that the Mafia is out to get Harry, who, so as not to detract from his reputation, continues to provoke violent deaths everywhere he goes.

Harry's research leads him to Jennifer Spence, a mysterious young woman who paints bizzare pictures and lives alone. Ten years earlier, in the company of her younger sister, Jennifer had been the victim of a revolting gang rape perpetrated by several of the town's inhabitants. Haunted by this nightmare in her past, Jennifer is carrying out a bloody and suicidal revenge.

Harry guesses the truth, but collides with Jannings, who seems to be covering for someone. Assisted by a young police officer whose life he has saved, Harry pursues his investigation to its conclusion, revealing, in a final erruption of violence, the ghosts of a past which everyone had wished to bury. And when he finally confronts Jennifer, who is both executioner and victim, Harry once more asks himself a question or two about that which we call justice.

In the eight years between *The Gauntlet* and *Sudden Impact* Eastwood had earnestly pursued his change of direction toward nonviolent characters and come up

takes a revolver out of her purse and fires into her partner's crotch before finishing him off with a bullet in the head.

That same morning finds Inspector Harry Callahan in a rotten mood. His testimony against a young hood named Hawkins was not accepted, and the judge just reprimanded him about his working methods, which are too cavalier in the strict eyes of the law. On his way back from court Harry stumbles upon an armed robbery at a coffeeshop he frequents. His day off to a swell start, Harry invites himself to the wedding of a famous mafioso's granddaughter and threatens the gangster, who succumbs to a fatal heart attack on the spot. Finally, to top things off, Harry is attacked by Hawkins and his buddies that same night, and, after a frenetic chase, Hawkins et al. wind up dead.

Weary of the cadavers that Harry leaves in his wake and determined to protect him from the press which is taking a strong stand against police brutality, Harry's superiors decide to send him on assignment to San Paulo, a small town in Northern California. The man who had been murdered at dawn was originally from San Paulo. Harry finds himself in charge of the investigation.

Jannings, the local police chief, is none too

The director at the camera

with work as sensitive as *Bronco Billy* and *Honkytonk Man*. Had the commercial failure of the latter forced Eastwood to return to his proven formula? Was *Sudden Impact* the result of a compromise or even an abandonment? Had he given in and given up? Such were the questions one could legitimately ask when the fourth Dirty Harry project was announced. From another point of view, returning to the character of Harry was a challenge for the producer-director-star—a challenge met with considerable flair, if one judges by its enormous success in the United States. Eastwood's decision to return to the role is a sound one essentially because *Sudden Impact* does not content itself with being a rehash of

the preceeding films, but branches out toward the baroque and lyrical. As in *High Plains Drifter,* Eastwood is willfully provocative at the beginning of the film. With devastating humor he shows us a Harry who has aged but is "dirtier" than ever. This man is a dinosaur and he knows it. He hasn't changed, but he has an excuse: The world around him hasn't exactly changed for the better either.

Eastwood reincarnates the character who made him famous, toys with his own myth, and has a good time at it. After all, Eastwood himself says that he now knows Harry so well that he can guess what his reaction might be in any number of given situations.

But once the viewer is on familiar ground, the di-

165

With Pat Hingle

rector introduces new elements, changes the style of narration, and heads into a tale that borders on the fantastic. First he eliminates Harry's habitual stomping ground and ships him off to a small provincial town. Then he makes his character more the hunted than the hunter. And finally he survives a nearly-fatal plunge before reappearing as would a phantom. When at the end, Harry returns from the land of limbo, he appears as an immortal specter, face in the shadows (a projector situated behind outlines his ghostly silhouette), indestructible, gun in hand. From that point on the violence can explode lyrically as in any other work of fantasy. Harry joins up with his mythic double from the end of *High Plains Drifter*, taking his leave of a town renamed "Hell" and re-painted red, without a backward glance for those who remain to carve the names on the headstones. . . .

With Fritz Manes, his executive producer

City Heat

1984

Distribution: Warner
Producer: Warner/Malpaso/Deliverance; Fritz Manes
Unit Production Manager: Fritz Manes
Director: Richard Benjamin
Screenplay: Sam O. Brown and Joseph C. Stinson, based on a story by Sam O. Brown
Director of Photography: Nick McLean (Technicolor/Panavision)
Art Director: Edward Carfango
Film Editor: Jacqueline Cambas
Music: Lennie Niehaus
First Assistant Director: David Valdes
Property Master: George Gaines
Sound Special Editors: Alan Robert Murray, Bob Henderson, Bob Asman, Gordon Davidson
Music Editing: Donald Harris (Dolby)
Script Supervisor: Marrie Kenney
Costumes: Norman Salling, Glenn Wright, Arlene Encell

Special Effects: Joe Unsinn
Transportation Captain: Donald R. Casella
Hairdresser: Barbara Lampson
Assistant to Mr. Benjamin: Carolyn Bauer
Length: 98 minutes

CAST:
Clint Eastwood: *Lieutenant Speer;* Burt Reynolds: *Mike Murphy;* Jane Alexander: *Addy;* Madeline Kahn: *Caroline Howley;* Rip Torn: *Primo Pitt;* Irene Cara: *Ginny Lee;* Richard Roundtree: *Dehl Swift;* Tony Lo Bianco: *Leon Coll;* William Sanderson: *Lonnie Ash;* Nicholas Worth: *Troy Roker;* Robert Davi: *Nino;* Jude Farese: *Dub Slack;* John Hancock: *Fat Freddie;* Tab Thacker: *Tuck;* Gerald S. O'Loughlin: *Counterman Louie;* Bruce M. Fischer, Art La Fleur: *bruisers;* Jack Nance: *Aram Strossell;* Dallas Cole: *Redhead Sherry;* Lou Filippo: *referee;* Michael Maurer: *Vint Diestock;* Preston Sparks: *Keith Stoddard;* Ernie Sabella: *ballistics expert;* Christopher Michael Moore: *Roxy cop;* Carey Loftin: *Roxy driver;* Harry Caesar: *locker room attendant;* Charles Parks: *Dr. Breslin;* Hamilton Camp: *garage attendant;* Jack Thibeau, Gene LeBell, Nick Dimitri, George Fisher, Bob Herron, Bill Hart:

With Burt Reynolds

169

garage soldiers; Arthur Malet: *Doc Loomis;* Fred Lerner: *Pitt roof sniper;* George Orrison: *Pitt doorway thug;* Beau Starr: *Pitt lookout;* Anthony Charnota, Walter Robles, Richard Foronjy: *poker players;* Joan Shawlee: *Peggy Barker;* Minnie Lindsey: *bordello maid;* Darwyn Swalve: *bordello bouncer;* Wiley Harker, Bob Maxwell: *"Mr. Smiths";* Tom Spratley: *chauffeur;* Bob Terhune: *billiard soldier;* Holgie Forrester: *Little Red;* Harry Demopoulos, M.D.: *Roman orgy patron;* Jim Lewis: *Roxy patron;* Edwin Prevost: *butler;* Alfie Wise: *short guy;* Hank Calia: *shorter friend;* Alex Plasschaert: *shortest friend;* Daphne Eckler: *Agnes;* Lonna Montrose: *Didi;* Michael Cassidy, Vincent Deadrick, Jr., Richard Drown, Bud Ekinds, Allan Graf, Chuck Hicks, Julius Le Flore, Fritz Manes, Debby Porter, James Hooks Reynolds, Mic Rodgers, Sharon Schaffer, Wayne Van Horn, Chuck Waters, George Wilbur, Glenn Wilder: *stuntmen*

The setting is Kansas City, the year 1933. Lieutenant Speer doesn't like cops who trade in their badges for a private detectives' licenses. And he doesn't much care for private detectives who are friendly with gangsters. In short, he doesn't like Mike Murphy, and if Murphy runs into trouble, Speer waits until the last possible moment to come to his rescue. Murphy's business is far from flourishing. His secretary Addy hasn't been paid for three months, and his associate, Dehl Swift, has a knack for getting Murphy into embarrassing situations. One day Swift shows up at the office with enough cash to cover back rent and Addy's salary. What is to all appearances a good deal is just the start of their troubles. Dehl has tried to pit two underworld kingpins, Primo Pitt and Leon Coll, against each other. When Dehl's subterfuge is discovered, it's Murphy's skin they want.

Speer hasn't given Murphy an inch. He still can't be certain of Murphy's honesty and begins to wonder whether he shouldn't just nab him along with the two gangsters. Despite everything, Speer has a certain amount of respect for Murphy, and is not immune to the charms of his loyal secretary. But he has other fish to fry: Ginny Lee, a speakeasy chanteuse who has the misfortune to be Dehl Swift's girlfriend, which fact has caused her to witness a murder. Ginny has become an underworld target, and both Speer and Murphy hope they can get to her before the killers.

Murphy's troubles are far from over, however. The gangsters have found another of his vulnerable points—his upper-crust girlfriend, Caroline Howley.

With Burt Reynolds

Murphy's going to find himself in quite a fix. Luckily for him, the gangsters make the mistake of infuriating the eminently irritable Lieutenant Speer. The two men follow the situation to its conclusion without diminishing their mutual antagonism one bit.

City Heat, originally entitled *Kansas City Blues,* was to have been directed by Blake Edwards. At the last minute the project fell to Richard Benjamin, a popular actor of the seventies (*Goodbye Columbus, Catch-22,* and *Westworld* are among his screen credits) who later became a theater and television director before turning to the cinema with *My Favorite Year* (1982) and *Racing with the Moon* (1984). An actor undoubtedly seemed like the perfect choice to handle the meeting of Clint Eastwood and Burt Reynolds, the two box-office idols *Time* magazine had dubbed the "Hollywood Honchos" some years earlier. Unfortunately, this long-awaited encounter didn't produce the fireworks anticipated. Although it was crafted with thorough attention to period detail and benefits from a terrific cast, *City Heat* suffers from a lack of rhythm and finesse. Hesitating between the serious and the cartoonish, Benjamin sacrifices the dramatic aspects of scenes in which scores are settled, in favor of spectacular special effects. Whereas the killings should merely punctuate this nostalgic homage to gangster movies of the thirties, the violence stops at nothing and every trick in the special effects book is tossed in for good measure under the general heading of pyrotechnics at all costs.

Nevertheless, Benjamin obviously loves actors and happily gives them free reign. Rip Torn and Tony Lo Bianco make delectable hoodlums, Richard Roundtree doesn't lack for dynamism, and the trio of women—Jane Alexander, Madeline Kahn, and Irene Cara—dispense liberal quantities of charm, humor, and seductiveness. As is usually the case in Eastwood films, particularly close attention has been paid to the soundtrack. Al Jarreau, Joe Williams, Irene

Cara, and Rudy Vallee sing melodies by Cole Porter and George and Ira Gershwin, among others, and Eastwood himself interprets the Lennie Niehaus tune ''Montage Blues'' at the piano, accompanied by Mike Lang and Pete Jolly.

The film's main attraction, of course, remains the teaming up of Eastwood and Reynolds. The two men's respective careers have many points in common: After difficult starts as bit players they made themselves known on TV, took a detour to Italy (Eastwood with Leone and Reynolds with Sergio Corbucci), and became stars via popular genres like the Western and the police thriller. Finally, both tried their hands at directing (with considerably more good fortune in Eastwood's case) and founded their own production companies, which are cited in the *City Heat* credits: Malpaso for Eastwood, Deliverance for Reynolds.

In *City Heat* the two stars toy with their images with plenty of humor. Reynolds demolishes his macho superhero persona by playing a ladies' man with slicked-down hair who has one hard break after another. As a cranky and incorruptible cop afflicted with nervous tics, Eastwood portrays a sort of paranoid Dirty Harry who knocks off gangsters in a style irresistibly reminiscent of the finales of the early Leone pictures. In short, the two actors enjoy themselves and show us a good time. But one can't help but think that their encounter would have been more explosive under the direction of Blake Edwards.

Tightrope

1984

Distribution: Warner
Producer: Warner/Clint Eastwood
Unit Production Manager: Fritz Manes
Director: Richard Tuggle
First Assistant Director: David Valdes
Screenplay: Richard Tuggle
Director Of Photography: Bruce Surtees (Technicolor/(Panavision)
Art Director: Ernie Bishop
Film Editor: Joel Cox
Music: Lennie Niehaus
Casting: Phyllis Huffman
Sound Editors: Alan Robert Murray, Gordon Davidson, Chet Slomka, Neil Burrow
Music Editor: Donald Harris
Dialogue Coach: Lloyd Nelson
Assistant Editor: John Morrisey
Transportation Coordinator: Bill Miller
Sound Mixing: William Kaplan
Boom Operator: Jules Strasser

Rerecording Mixers: Les Fresholtz, Dick Alexander, Vern Poore
Cameraman: Jack Green
Second Cameramen: John Walker, Leo Napolotano
Second Unit Cameraman: Billy Bragg
Stunt Coordinator: Wayne Van Horn
Key Grip: Charles Saldana
Assistant Grips: Bruce Spellman, Kirk E. Bales
Gaffer: Tom Stern
Assistant Gaffer: Victor Perez
Special Effects: Joe Unsinn
Still Photographer: Marsha Reed
Costumes: Glenn Wright
Dresser: Deborah Ann Hooper
Property Master: Eddie Aiona
Makeup: Barbara Guedel
Hairdresser: Marlene Williams
Production Secretary: Linda Sony Kinney
Length: 114 minutes

CAST:
Clint Eastwood: *Wes Block;* Genevieve Bujold: *Beryl Thibodeaux;* Dan Hedaya: *Inspector Molinary;* Alison Eastwood: *Amanda Block;* Jennifer Beck: *Penny Block;* Marco St. John: *Leandre;* Rebecca Pearle:

With Alison Eastwood

Becky Jacklin; Regina Richardson: *Sarita;* Randi Brooks: *Jamie Cory;* Jamie Rose: *Melanie Silber;* Margaret Howell: *Rudy Harper:* Rebecca Clemons: *woman with whip;* Jannet MacLachlan: *Dr. Yarlosky;* Graham Paul: *Luther;* Bill Holiday: *police chief;* John Wilmot: *forensic surgeon;* Margie O'Dair: *Mrs. Holstein;* Joy N. Houck, Jr.: *massage parlor owner;* Stuart Baker-Bergen: *surfer;* Donald Barber: *Shorty;* Robert Harvey: *Lonesome Alice;* Ron Gural: *investigator;* Layton Martens: *Sergeant Surtees;* Richard Charles Boyle: *Dr. Fitzpatrick;* Becki Davis: *nurse;* Jonathan Sacher: *male prostitute;* Valerie Thibodeaux: *prostitute;* Lionel Ferbos: *passerby;* Elliot Keener: *Sandoval;* Cary Wilmot Alden: *Secretary;* David Valdes: *Manes;* James Borders: *Carfagno;* Fritz Manes: *Valdes;* Jonathan Shaw: *Wuono;* Don Lutenbacher: *Brewery Director;* George Wood: *sales representative;* Kimberly Georgoulis: *Sam;* Glenda Byars: *Lucy Davis*

Since his wife walked out on him, Wes Block, homicide inspector for the New Orleans Police Department, lives alone with his two daughters, Amanda and Penny. A series of particularly ghastly murders has raised public indignation. Certain organizations lay the blame directly on the police, accusing them of ineffectiveness. This is the charge leveled by many members of the women's movement and particularly the lovely Beryl Thibodeaux, director of the city's rape crisis center.

Inspector Block's investigation is all the more delicate in light of the fact that the murderer is so sure of himself that he doesn't hesistate to provoke the police. What's more, Block himself is attracted by certain so-called "kinky" sexual practices and knew two of the murdered prostitutes personally. His investigation brings him into contact with other young women who specialize in the sort of pleasure he seeks. Some of his colleagues begin to wonder if Block isn't directly connected with the murders. Worse still, through a series of messages, the murderer lures Block to specific places where he's certain to find what he's looking for. So it is that Block finds himself in an establishment which caters to sadomasochists. Block then asks Beryl Thibodeaux for her help. But one night, while Wes and Beryl are out together, a prostitute Wes has patronized not long before is murdered. And, at the scene of the crime, in plain sight, is a necktie belonging to Block.

Block then understands that the killer is going to zero in and wants to put the blame on him. First he must see to it that his daughters are safely guarded. But the killer eludes police surveillance. When Block returns home he finds the baby-sitter murdered. He puts Penny in the closet for safety's sake and searches the house for his older daughter Amanda, whom he finds handcuffed and gagged on a bed.

The killer has now been identified thanks to clues left by his shoes. Block chases after him and the two men pin each other down in a bloody hand-to-hand fight. Block emerges victorious and stumbles away with Beryl at his side.

Written and directed by Richard Tuggle, *Tightrope* gives Eastwood an opportunity to try something new with his character in a film noir setting. Similar to the Dirty Harry of *Sudden Impact* in his skepticism and bitterness, the cop of *Tightrope* is nevertheless not hemmed in by his solitude. Separated from his wife, he has custody of his two daughters and even embarks on an affair with a militant feminist. More important yet, he is fascinated by the criminal's world to the extent that the viewer ends up asking himself whether the cop himself is not really the killer, and

this search for the guilty party, in the end, is a savage form of psychoanalysis. The watchword is ambiguity. Here it is no longer a question of determining whether or not such a thing as justice exists, but of understanding the reasons behind evil. Evil is horrible, but also fascinating, and echoes tellingly within he who is responsible for defending good.

Doubtless the presence of the three women who surround him has a great deal of bearing on the fact that the man on the tightrope ends up on the right side, the side of goodness and decency. Far from the sorts of heroes portrayed by Charles Bronson, who leans more and more toward the lone avenger, the typical Eastwood character knows moments of doubt, weakness, and defeat. His journey is one that leads to the end of night, a journey from which he can't help but emerge wounded and troubled. This fundamental

With Genevieve Bujold

179

ambiguity is that of film noir itself. Awareness of the significance of his actions dwindles in the eerie city night, and reactions owe as much to reflex as they do to reflection. The killer is the lawman's double and the final battle between the two can't help but bring to mind the combat between Dr. Jekyll and Mr. Hyde.

Pulling off a role of this kind is an attempt at the impossible for a star like Eastwood. Not only does he hesitate less than ever to put his image into question, but he goes so far as to shock the viewer by not offering the slightest psychological excuse for his character's behavior. The killer leaves Block clues and evidence because he alone truly knows, fully understands him. The killer is not so much bent on revenge as he is on pushing Block over into the shadowy underworld. Eastwood responded clearly when I asked him, "Do you think you'll cross the border one day and play a bad guy?" His answer: "Maybe. I've already played killers, but always within the limits of the law. Play a psychopathic killer someday? Sure, why not. That might be interesting."

Set for the most part at night, in a world of prostitutes and sexual perversion, particularly sado-masochism, *Tightrope* is a grim and violent film, a descent into hell which can legitimately conclude only in a bloody exorcism. Like that of *Sudden Impact,* the end here, with a rare brutality, takes us into the realm of the horror film and displays, in no uncertain terms, Eastwood's taste for the strange and the baroque—a predilection which is again apparent in *Pale Rider* and which should literally explode in the years to come.

With Richard Tuggle, the director

Pale Rider

1985

Distribution: Warner
Producer: Warner/Malpaso; Clint Eastwood
Executive Producer: Fritz Manes
Director: Clint Eastwood
First Assistant Director: David Valdes
Screenplay: Michael Butler and Dennis Shryack
Director of Photography: Bruce Surtees (Technicolor)
Art Director: Edward Carfango
Film Editor: Joel Cox
Associate Producer: David Valdes
Unit Production Manager: Fritz Manes
Music: Lennie Niehaus
Casting: Phyllis Huffman
Set Decorator: Ernie Bishop
Script Supervisor: Lloyd Nelson
Sound Effects Editing Supervision: Alan Robert Murray and Bob Henderson (Dolby)
Music Editing: Donald Harris
Rerecording mixer: C. Darin Knight
Stunt Coordinator: Wayne Van Horn
Length: 113 minutes

CAST:

Clint Eastwood: *the preacher;* Michael Moriarty: *Hull Barret;* Carrie Snodgress: *Sarah Wheeler;* Christopher Penn: *Josh LaHood;* Richard Dysart: *Coy LaHood;* Sydney Penny: *Megan Wheeler;* Richard Kiel: *Club;* Doug McGrath: *Spider Conway;* John Russell: *Stockburn;* Charles Hallahan: *McGill;* Marvin J. McIntyre: *Jagou;* Frank Ryan: *Matt Blakenship;* Richard Hamilton: *Jed Blakenship;* Graham Paul: *Ev Gossage;* Chuck LaFont: *Eddie Conway* Jeffrey Weissman: *Teddy Conway;* Allen Keller: *Tyson;* Tom Oglesby: *Elam;* Herman Poppe: *Ulrik Lindquist;* Kathleen Wygle: *Bess Gossage;* Terrence Evans: *Jake Henderson;* Jim Hitson: *Biggs;* Loren Adkins: *Bossy;* Tom Friedkin: *Miner Tom;* S. A. Griffin, Billy Drago, Jeffrey Josephson, John Dennis Johnston: *Deputies*

With the help of his son Josh and his hired men, Coy LaHood sees that his word is law in the town that bears his name. LaHood is at the head of a mining trust which extracts minerals with hydraulic equipment that will eventually wear out the soil. He's trying to get rid of a group of independent miners and gold seekers operating on what he considers to be "his" territory. The independents, installed in the reportedly mineral-rich vicinity of Carbon Canyon, are led by Hull Barrett, his fiancée Sarah Wheeler, and her daughter Megan. Coy LaHood dispatches a group of armed men to sack the encampment so as to aid the undesirables in reaching their decision to move out.

In the course of their expedition LaHood's men kill Megan's dog. The adolescent buries her pet and prays to the lord above to come to their aid. It is then that a mysterious horseman in a preacher's cloak appears on a pale horse. The stranger rides into town at the very moment that Hull, who has come to town to stock up on supplies to rebuild his camp, finds himself in a tough spot with LaHood's men. The stranger intervenes in Hull's favor and rides back along with him as far as Carbon Canyon.

Seeing that he's failed to intimidate the independents, LaHood hires the services of a marshal named Stockburn, who shows up with six deputies to carry out the job. For his part, the stranger lets the independents fall back on their own resources by explaining to them what the consequences of their resistance are likely to be. The independents decide to stay but quickly realize that their chances of winning are slim indeed. The stranger then rides into town on his pale horse and confronts Stockburn and his men. At the moment of the final showdown Stockburn recognizes the preacher, whose path he has crossed once before.

"And I saw, and behold, a pale horse, and its rider's name was death, and hell followed him." It is at the very moment that she recites this eighth verse from chapter six of Revelations in the King James Bible that young Megan witnesses the appearance of a stranger on a pale horse. After a classic beginning (LaHood's men ambushing the miner's camp) opulently shot, the appearance of the "preacher," incarnated by Clint Eastwood, clearly states the auteur's intentions. His character is a horseman of the Apocalypse, come from nothingness like the "high plains drifter" before him, and carrying, as did the drifter, a scar, which will be explained in the end.

There is one slight difference. The high plains drifter was full of contempt and scorn for the town of cowards which had abandoned him to be brutally murdered. The "pale rider" has come to help a community in need. He becomes a part of it for the length of his stay. Revenge will come as a bonus. The stranger's back is marred by the traces of bullet wounds. Stockburn killed him once upon a time. And he will kill Stockburn in the very same way, cutting him down at point blank range; it is at the moment that the bullets exit from Stockburn's back, having pierced his body, that the viewer understands the significance of the scars the stranger carries. And he also understands that the preacher, like the high plains drifter, is a phantom who will disappear, this time for good, into the mists of eternity.

This new character confirms Eastwood's taste for supernatural. "In the beginning there was the conflict

184

between the independent miners and the all-powerful trust,'' he explains. ''To develop the biblical parallels I ended up accentuating the supernatural aspect a bit.'' An aspect which he would reinforce through the introduction of the marshal. ''When it was a question of my character, I felt that we had to create a relationship in his past with an antagonist, the Sheriff. That way the figure of the Stranger takes on an extra dimension. And it also goes along with the idea of the horseman of the Apocalypse.''[1]

But *Pale Rider* is much more grounded in American history than was *High Plains Drifter*. It evokes the pioneer experience, the struggle of independent miners against a trust, and, by extension, the assorted struggles which bloodied the West: land barons and their enormous ranches versus colonies of immigrants, cattlemen versus shepherds, etc. Seen from this angle, the film marks a reconciliation between the classic Western with its positive values) the defense of liberty, solidarity, the rights of the oppressed) and the cinema of baroque allegory. Eastwood has resurrected an American genre par excellence, respecting the rules but at the same time making the form his own by imposing his personal obsessions. *Pale Rider* is, above all, *film d'auteur*.

As for its execution, *Pale Rider* is striking in its plastic beauty. The vibrant lyricism of nature and the exteriors contrasts sharply with the shadowy obscurity of interiors shot with a minimum of light. If one adds that the work was completed in five and a half weeks, one fully understands the extent to which Clint Eastwood has mastered the art of producton and the craft of directing.

1. Interview with Michael Henry, taken from Cannes Film Festival press kit for *Pale Rider*.

ABOVE: With Shirley MacLaine in Don Siegel's Two Mules for Sister Sara

OPPOSITE, TOP: With Sondra Locke in Bronco Billy

OPPOSITE, BOTTOM: With Rada Rassimov in Sergio Leone's The Good, the Bad and the Ugly

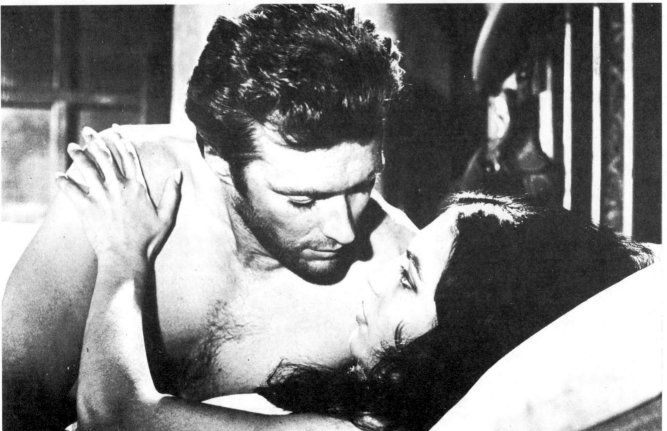

OPPOSITE, TOP: With Stella Garcia in John Sturges' Joe Kidd

OPPOSITE, BOTTOM: With Jean Seberg in Joshua Logan's Paint Your Wagon

ABOVE: With Marianne Hill in High Plains Drifter

OPPOSITE, TOP: With Sondra Locke in The Gauntlet

OPPOSITE, BOTTOM: With Marianne Koch in Sergio Leone's A Fistful of Dollars

ABOVE: With Ingrid Pitt in Brian G. Hutton's Where Eagles Dare

Clint Eastwood's Bronco Billy

BIBLIOGRAPHY

Books

Agan, Patrick. *Clint Eastwood: The Man Behind the Myth*. London: Robert Hale, 1977.

Downing, David, and Gary Herman. *Clint Eastwood: All-American Anti-Hero*. New York: Omnibus Press, 1977.

Ferrari, Philippe. *Clint Eastwood*. Paris: Solar, 1980.

Frank, Alan. *Clint Eastwood*. London: Optimum Books, 1982.

Kaminsky, Stuart. *Clint Eastwood*. New York: New American Library, 1974.

Whitman, Mark. *The Films of Clint Eastwood*. Isle of Wight: BCW, 1973.

Zmijewsky, Boris, and Lee Pfeiffer. *The Films of Clint Eastwood*. Secaucus, N.J.: Citadel Press, 1982.

Articles and Interviews

Garnier, Philippe. "Notre homme Clint." *Rock et Folk,* no. 172, May 1981.

Guérif, François. "Clint Eastwood." *La Revue du Cinéma,* no. 335, Jan. 1979.

Hadenfield, Chris. "Clint Eastwood: 'Let's Go to Lunch and BS for a While.'" *Look,* July 1979.

Knight, Arthur. "A Candid Conversation with Clint Eastwood." *Playboy,* Feb. 1974.

McGilligan, Patrick. "Interview with Clint Eastwood." *Focus on Film,* no. 25, Summer/Fall 1976.

Merigeau, Pascal. "Eastwood derrière la caméra." *La Revue du Cinéma,* no. 335, Jan. 1979.

Mitchell, Steve. "Escape from Alcatraz: An Interview with Director Don Siegel," *Filmmakers,* June 1979.

Schickel, Richard. "Good Ole Burt; Cool Eyed Clint." *Time,* Jan. 9, 1978.

Zimmer, Jacques. "Eastwood et la critique française." *La Revue du Cinéma,* no. 335, Jan. 1979.